Get to the Point!

Writing Effective Email, Letters, Memos, Reports, and Proposals

Ron Blicq and Lisa Moretto
RGI International

Prentice Hall Allyn and Bacon Canada
Scarborough, Ontario

Canadian Cataloguing in Publication Data

Blicq, Ron S. (Ron Stanley, 1925 –
    Get to the Point!

Includes index.
ISBN 0-13-020420-X

1. Business writing. 2. Business communication. 3. Business report writing. 4. Electronic mail
messages. 5. Business presentations. I. Moretto, Lisa A. II. Title. III. Get to the Point!

HF5718.3.B54   2000   808'.06665   C99-932521-0

Prentice-Hall, Inc., Upper Saddle River, New Jersey
Prentice-Hall International (UK) Limited, London
Prentice-Hall of Australia, Pty. Limited, Sydney
Prentice-Hall Hispanoamericana, S.A., Mexico City
Prentice-Hall of India Private Limited, New Delhi
Prentice-Hall of Japan, Inc., Tokyo
Simon & Schuster Southeast Asia Private Limited, Singapore
Editora Prentice-Hall do Brasil, Ltda., Rio de Janeiro

ISBN 0-13-020420-X

Vice-President, Editorial Director: Laura Pearson
Acquisitions Editor: David Stover
Executive Developmental Editor: Marta Tomins
Associate Editor: Susan Ratkaj
Copy Editor: Melanie M. Meharchand
Production Editor: Melanie M. Meharchand
Production Coordinator: Peggy Brown
Art Director: Mary Opper
Cover Image: PhotoDisc

41 16

Printed and bound in Canada.

Visit the Prentice Hall Canada web site! Send us your comments, browse our catalogues, and
more at **www.phcanada.com**. Or reach us through e-mail at **phabinfo_pubcanada@prenhall.com**.

Contents

Preface

When we talk to practitioners — business people, administrators, engineers, architects, medical specialists, and so on — they all tell us the same thing: "Show me some techniques I can use to write more efficiently. Give me something short, that I can dip into when I have to write a difficult letter or comprehensive report."

So, this is strictly a "how-to" book in which we present techniques you can adopt when you have to write email, an informative letter or report, or a persuasive proposal. In particular, it will help you when you have to convince a reader to act on your suggestions or recommendations. Whether you are already working — and writing — in the real world, or are still in school preparing for it, this book will provide the techniques you need to make your letters, memos, emails, and reports clear, concise, and effective.

In Chapter 1 we show you how to overcome writer's block by using the Pyramid Method. Then, in Chapters 2 through 5, we show you how to develop the pyramid into a writing plan that organizes your information coherently, regardless of what you have to write. There is a different writing plan for each type of letter, report, and proposal. You will also find numerous examples you can use as models when planning and writing your own documents. In particular, the models demonstrate how the Pyramid Method can be applied to every document, whether it's a short email message, a one-page letter or memorandum, a five-page report, or a fifty-page proposal.

Chapter 6 shows you how to design a report or proposal to increase its readability and direct a reader's attention to key information. It also introduces you to techniques for eliminating gender-specific language and for writing to readers in other cultures — an essential skill in our increasingly global marketplace.

Finally, Chapter 7 suggests ways to sharpen the words you use and the sentences you write so they are direct and definite, neither too abrupt nor too wordy, and give your readers confidence in you as an effective conveyor of information. Chapter 7 also includes self-test exercises so you can test the skills you have learned.

We expect that, when you want to learn how to write a particular type of letter, report, memo, email, or proposal, you will want to go straight to the chapter and section that gives the advice you need. We suggest, however, that before you start searching for specific advice, you first read Chapters 1 and 2. They will introduce you to the writer's pyramid and show you how to apply it in letter-writing situations. This will help you later, when you want to use the Pyramid Method to structure longer reports and proposals.

We particularly want to thank the editors at Prentice Hall Canada, who kept "reminding" us of our approaching manuscript submission deadline and, once the manuscript was "in-house," kept it moving along. And we especially appreciated the help of Elizabeth Pierce, who was our personal editor and stitched our different chapters into a coherent whole.

L.M. and R.B.

About the Authors

Ron Blicq and Lisa Moretto are Senior Consultants with RGI International, a consulting company specializing in oral and written communication. They teach workshops based on the Pyramid Method of Writing, presented in this book, to audiences all over the world.

Ron is Senior Consultant of RGI's Canadian office. He has extensive experience as a technical writer and editor with the Royal Air Force in Britain and CAE Industries Limited in Canada, and has been teaching technical and business communication since 1967. Ron has authored five books with Prentice Hall and has written and produced six educational video programs including *Sharpening Your Business Communication Skills* and *So, You Have to Give a Talk?* He is a Fellow of both the Society for Technical Communication and the Association of Teachers of Technical Writing, and is a Life Member of the Institute of Electrical and Electronics Engineers Inc. Ron lives in Winnipeg, Manitoba. In the summer he flies with the Winnipeg Gliding Club; in the winter he has been learning to downhill ski.

Lisa is Senior Consultant of RGI's United States' office. She has experience as an Information Developer for IBM in the U.S. and as a Learning Products Engineer for Hewlett-Packard in the U.K. Lisa holds a B.Sc. in Technical Communication from Clarkson University, New York, and an M.Sc. in User Interface Design from London Guildhall University. Her specialties include developing online interactive information, designing user interfaces, and writing product documentation. She is a member of both the Society for Technical Communication and the Institute of Electrical and Electronics Engineers Inc. Lisa lives in Myrtle Beach, South Carolina. Although she lives by the ocean, Lisa's heart is in the mountains for she is an ardent skier.

Photo courtesy of Mary Lou Stein

CHAPTER 1

Getting Started

If you are like most people, you find it difficult to start a writing project. It doesn't matter if it's a one-page memo to your staff, a complaint letter, or a formal proposal. You stare at the computer screen or the blank page and wait for inspiration. Or you pour a cup of coffee or stroll around the office, but neither seems to bring inspiration. You know you are wasting your time *and* the company's money. It's frustrating.

When you do finally settle down and start writing, you may find that your words come easily and seem to flow. Sometimes though, the words flow too easily and you may end up rambling. This is what we call a "brain dump," and the result is often a very confusing, unorganized piece of rhetoric. You've probably received information written like this. As you read it, you keep wondering when the writer is going to get to the point. And if you happen to read the whole message, you still may not be sure what is expected of you.

This is just one of many common problems writers have. You're not alone. We're going to introduce you to some techniques we've been teaching people for over 20 years. They will help you become a quicker, more effective writer by showing you how to

- identify the audience,
- identify the primary information,
- focus the reader's attention on the primary information,
- get started,
- understand the difference between *tell* and *sell* messages, and
- learn to structure your writing.

Identifying the Audience

Before you sit down to write *anything*, you need to know who you are writing to and what they need to know from you. This is one of the most common problems people have when they try to communicate information — they haven't properly identified their audience.

You need to ask yourself some questions about your reader. Often you will know exactly who you are writing to, in which case it is relatively easy to identify what information that particular person (or people) wants or needs from you. In some cases you may have communicated with the person before. However, there will be other times when you will not personally know your reader, and on these occasions you have to identify the *type* of person (or people) who will be reading your writing. This may occur if, for example, you are writing operating instructions for a new software program or responding to a Request for Proposal for a government contract.

Ask Questions

When you have a reader in mind, ask yourself five specific questions about that person:

1. What does my reader want to know?

2. What does my reader need to be told?

    There may be a significant difference between what a reader would like to hear and what a reader needs to hear (as in the case of a client who expects you to report that a job is complete, and who has to be told that it is not).

3. What does my reader already know about this subject?

    Understanding what he or she knows about the subject will help you identify where to start and how much background information to include.

4. Who else is likely to read my letter or report?

    There may be secondary readers to whom the document will be circulated and you need to identify their knowledge level and interests, too.

5   If there is more than one reader, who will make a decision based on the information I'm writing?

    The person making the decision(s) will be your primary reader. This will also be the person to whom you direct the key information.

Identifying your audience will not only help you direct your message but it will also help you choose the most appropriate tone and language.

Focus the Message

Once you identify who you are writing to and what they most need to know from you, you have to position that information so it gets the attention it deserves. At school, we were taught to use the "climactic" method of writing that encouraged us to write all our facts down first, before we could make our main point. This allowed the reader to understand all the events or circumstances that led up to the main message. Usually the points were listed chronologically.

As adults, we are still influenced by our education and often still write in the climactic style. Unfortunately, this method isn't appropriate for business communications. This is apparent in how Alan Cairns, Vancourt Business Systems' chief purchasing agent, described an order mix-up in a memo to senior accountant Liz Watson (see Figure 1–1).

Although Liz will understand what the situation is and what Alan is trying to tell her, she has to read the entire message before she learns that something is expected of her. In today's hectic business environment, we are often interrupted by the telephone, meetings, or someone needing our attention. Alan has taken the risk that Liz may be interrupted and may not read to the end of his message. She may never understand that she has to take an action.

Alan would have been better off if he had identified the main message for Liz — the most important information — and placed it right up front. That way, Liz would know his reason for writing right at the beginning. We call this the "immediate" method of writing.

Figure 1–2 graphically compares the climactic and immediate methods of writing. Notice the amount of time it takes for the reader to get to the main message in each.

To use the immediate method, Alan must first identify his audience, which means asking himself these questions:

1. **Who is my reader?**
    Liz Watson, senior accountant

2. **What does she already know about the situation?**
    Very little, except that she has a copy of the original purchase order (No. 41258)

3. **What does she most want or need to know?**
    She has to alter her copy of PO 41258 by changing the quantity ordered and the total dollar figure.

With the information gained from this quick audience analysis, Alan is ready to rewrite his memo to Liz. This time he puts the main message in the first paragraph:

To correct an ordering error, please change the quantity only and total amount entries on PO 41258 from "1" to "2," and "$267.80" to "$535.60." This will make our purchase order agree with Cardorinth Importers' invoice No. 2253.

If you place this main message at the beginning of Alan's original memo, you will notice the memo makes much more sense. When you know Alan's reason for writing, you don't have to keep wondering, "Why am I reading this?" Liz will know exactly what's expected of her after reading the first paragraph. Also, with the main information right up front, Alan can edit out many of the details he previously included, which will result in a much shorter, more concise memo.

Figure 1-1   A memo using the climactic method

Liz:

On September 5, I ordered a case of spindles from Cardorinth Importers for $267.80. The purchase order number was 41258. When, a week later, the Assembly Department said their need was urgent, I telephoned Cardorinth and asked them to expedite the order. As a precaution, I followed up with an email message on September 13 asking them to send it to me overnight.

Unfortunately, my email quoted an erroneous PO number (41528 instead of 41258), which Cardorinth treated as a second order. This second order arrived first, on September 19, and was accepted by the Material Control Department as belonging to PO 41258 without the discrepancy in purchase order numbers being noticed.

Then, when the original order eventually arrived on September 26, it also was accepted by Material Control. The Assembly Department has since used parts from both shipments, so we cannot return either of them.

Because we have used PO number 41528 for another order to a different supplier, I have authorized Cardorinth Importers to invoice us for both cases of spindles against PO number 41258. So will you please change the quantity to "2 cases" and the amount to "$535.60" on your copy of the purchase order, and pay Cardorinth $535.60 against their invoice No. 2253.

Alan

Figure 1-2 A graphical comparison of climactic vs. immediate method of writing

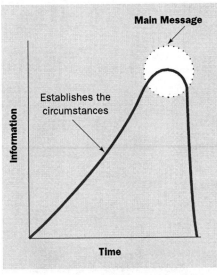

The climactic method of writing

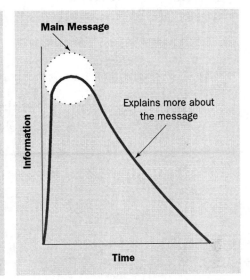

The immediate method of writing

Divide the Information

Once you decide what the main message is, you then need to decide what details are necessary to support that message. In Alan's case he needs to ask himself: "If I was Liz, what else would I want to know after reading the main message?", to which he might reply:

1. What caused the error?

2. Why do the changes need to be made and what effect will they have?

The answers to these questions become the supporting details and are placed immediately following the main message. You can visualize this information in two distinct blocks:

The main message (from now on we refer to it as the Summary Statement) is what the reader most needs to know. The Supporting Details answer any questions the reader may have after reading the Summary Statement: *What? Who? When? Where? Why? How?*

In Figure 1–3, Alan's memo to Liz has been rewritten using the immediate method. The first paragraph contains the Summary Statement and the remaining paragraphs give the Supporting Details. Using these

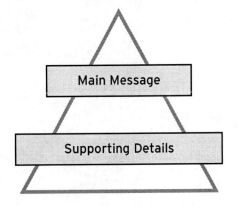

compartments as building blocks helps you construct clear, concise, and effective memos, letters, reports, and email messages. In later chapters we'll expand the compartments and adapt them to various situations.

Figure 1-3   Using writing compartments to structure a memo

Liz:

Summary
Statement

To correct an ordering error, please change the quantity and total amount entries on PO 41258 from "1" to "2," and "$267.80" to "$535.60." This will make our purchase order agree with Cardorinth Importers' invoice number 2253.

Supporting
Details

The error occurred when we inadvertently referred to PO 41528 (instead of 41258) in an email message to Cardorinth, which they interpreted as an additional order for spindles. The error was compounded twice: first by Material Control, which accepted both shipments against PO 41258, and then by Assembly, which opened and used parts from both shipments.

To avoid further complications (and because we have used PO number 41528 to purchase goods from a different supplier), I have authorized Cardorinth Importers to transfer the order for spindles they supplied against PO 41528 onto PO 41258, and to invoice us for both shipments on the one order.

Alan

Finding the Words to Start

Most people prefer to read letters that have the main message right up front because they are easier to understand and simplify their work. Some writers, however, have difficulty finding the right words to formulate their opening sentences. To overcome this difficulty, imagine your reader is right in front of you and has asked: "What do you *most* want to tell me?" When you answer that question you will have identified your main message or Summary Statement.

To help you find the right words we suggest that, before you start writing, you first jot down these six words,

I want to tell you that...

and then finish the sentence. For example,

I want to tell you that, **starting November 8, all staff must register their software with the Information Technology Department.**

Once you finish writing the sentence, delete the six introductory words. We call them the "six hidden words." Your new opening sentence is:

Starting November 8, all staff must register their software with the Information Technology Department.

If you use this technique each time you write a memo, letter, report, or email message, it will help you to start writing quickly; it will also ensure the main message is at the beginning. Figure 1–4 shows more examples of opening sentences.

Figure 1-4   Examples of opening sentences for business letters and memos

I want to tell you that...

- Our purchase order No. W1143 has been cancelled.
- Louise McKenzie will be representing Floral West Imports Ltd. at the Western Purchasing Agents' meeting on November 6.
- We have experienced numerous breakdowns with the BX-7 box stapler we purchased from you and request that you replace it with a more reliable model.
- Your order was shipped air express on May 15 and you should have received it the following morning.
- Our customs brokers have received only three of the four cartons listed on waybill C2827 and will not clear the shipment until they receive the fourth carton.

Sometimes your Summary Statement may seem too abrupt or impolite when the six hidden words are removed. For example,

Dear Ms. Darwin:

Your June 10 order for 80 ceramic flower holders cannot be filled until mid-October.

In a situation like this you need some additional words to soften the unwanted message so it isn't so abrupt.

Dear Ms. Darwin:

I regret that **your June 10 order for 80 ceramic flower holders cannot be filled until mid-October.**

If you phrase your Summary Statement as a question or a direct instruction, the six hidden words won't work. However, using these techniques is another way to force the main message into the first paragraph. For example,

May I have your approval to attend a one-week management training course at the University of Manitoba from March 10 to 14?

Can you install a staircase between area K7 and our administration area immediately above it?

Please cancel our purchase order W1143, dated May 5.

Avoid False Starts

A false start uses wasteful, unnecessary words that make it seem like you are "spinning your wheels." We see so many other people use them in their writing that we tend, almost automatically, to insert them as the openings to our memos, letters, and email messages. We call them false starts because they draw you into a long, convoluted sentence that is difficult to understand and difficult to punctuate properly. For example,

Dear Mr. Kosty:

With reference to your letter of November 19, in which you describe the discolouration of our paint colour No. 188 when used as a second coat on top of primer No. 145, we have conducted an investigation into your problem. Our conclusion is that the paint you used may have exceeded its shelf life.

Notice how "*I want to tell you that…*" doesn't work with this opening sentence. You cannot place it at the beginning and create a coherent sentence. If the opening had started like this, it would be more focused and concise:

Dear Mr. Kosty:

We have investigated the problem of paint discolouration described in your November 19 letter, and have concluded that the paint you used may have exceeded its shelf life.

Now you can place "*I want to tell you that...*" at the beginning of the sentence.

An Unimaginative, Directionless Start

Here are more examples of false starts and some warnings!

- Never start with a word that ends in "-ing":

  Referring...

  Replying...

- Never start with an expression that ends with the preposition "to":

  With reference to...

  In answer to...

  Pursuant to...

  Due to...

The "-ing" words and "to" phrases may cause you to ramble and punctuate incorrectly. The "to" phrase in the first letter to Mr. Kosty creates a rambling introductory sentence.

- Never start with a redundant expression:

  I am writing...

  For your information...

  This is to inform you...

  The purpose of this letter is...

  We have received your letter...

A reader can *see* that you are writing, *knows* you are writing to impart information, and is aware that you wouldn't be replying if you *hadn't* received his or her letter.

- Never send the reader on a hunt:

  Enclosed please find...

  Attached herewith...

If you say it's *attached*, it's redundant to also say it's *here*. Try writing simply:

  Here is...

  Attached is...

A Strong, Focused Start

Always remember the "six hidden words":

I want to tell you that...

If you consistently open each memo, letter, or email message with these words (and later delete them), you will never again make a false start. Whenever you write a memo, letter, or email message, test your opening sentence by inserting the six hidden words to see if your opening makes sense.

Identifying Your Purpose for Writing

We've already discussed the importance of identifying your audience or reader, but before you start writing, you also need to answer one more question: "What is the purpose of this communication?" People often answer with vague statements like:

- I have to report on the progress of our index-conversion program.
- I want more storage space, so I am asking for an additional filing cabinet.
- I need approval to send two of my staff to a proposal-writing course.

These responses show the writers are more concerned with their own needs than with the reader's needs. The writers have not identified *what they want their readers to do.*

Before you pick up your pen or place your hands on your computer keyboard, decide what kind of message you want to convey. There are only two to choose from:

- Messages that *tell* about facts and events. (Informative writing)
- Messages that *sell* an idea or a concept. (Persuasive writing)

Tell Messages

Communications that *tell* are primarily *informative:* they simply pass along information and do not expect the reader to respond. Consequently, they need to be clear, concise, and definite. Because tell messages refer to tangibles (facts, events, occurrences, and happenings), you can get straight to the point and describe only the essential details. A tell message can also be an instruction that directs somebody to do something.

After reading a tell message the reader's reaction is simply to say or mentally comment, "OK, that's interesting. Now I know."

Sell Messages

Communications that *sell* have to be *persuasive:* they present an idea or concept and require the reader to act or react, by agreeing with, approving, or implementing the idea, suggestion, or proposal. Consequently, if your reader is to react in the way you want, your communication must be *convincing*.

Because sell messages refer to intangibles (ideas, concepts, suggestions, and proposals), you must develop the background and details in sufficient depth to ensure that the reader has all the information he or she needs to make a decision or to take the appropriate action. You should, though, avoid presenting too much information, which might make your message obscure.

First you need to decide your purpose for writing and the response you want from your reader. Ask yourself:

- Am I *requesting* something?
- Am I *proposing* that something be done?
- Do I want *approval* to do something?

After reading a sell message, the reader's reaction might be something like, "You have a good point! I'll get right to it." If you have written an effective opening with the main message right up front, the reader of a sell message *knows exactly what response is expected.*

Examples of Tell and Sell Messages

Here are two messages: one is a tell and one is a sell. In both situations Richard is writing to his manager.

Tell Message

Dear Susan:

The RMF project is currently three days behind schedule, but we will make up the time and be back on schedule by March 1. We will be able to deliver the project to the client on the planned April 13 date.

We had two engineers absent because of an illness for two weeks and an equipment failure set us back two days. The JCT group was able to lend us one of their computers while ours was being repaired. Each member of the team is able to work three hours overtime each week for the next two weeks, which will ensure that we are back on schedule by March 1.

Richard

Richard does not expect a response from Susan. The purpose of this message is to simply inform her of the delay and to explain what will be done to get the project back on schedule.

Sell Message

Dear Susan:

The RMF project is currently three days behind schedule and unless we receive your approval to transfer one engineer and one computer to us, we will not be able to deliver the project to the client on April 13, as promised.

We had two engineers absent because of illness for two weeks and an equipment failure set us back two days. To make up this lost time we need an engineer and a computer transferred from the JCT project to the RMF project for three weeks.

Please let me know by February 13 if you approve this request so I can begin working on the transfer and reschedule the engineers' assignments.

Richard

In this case Richard needs a response and has told Susan exactly what he wants: her approval to transfer an engineer and a computer.

One major problem with requests and proposals is that writers tend to tell when they need to sell. For example, Carol Winters, a personnel manager, wants to correct the problem of long, time-wasting lineups at the lunchroom counter by staggering lunch hours between departments. Here's the first memo she wrote:

Dear Supervisors:

Starting May 28, I want you to delay the start of the lunch hour for employees in your department until 12:30 p.m.

Carol

Although her memo is clear and concise, many supervisors might resist the change because they don't understand why she is making the request. Because she needs their cooperation for her plan to work, she has to make sure the supervisors fully understand what she is trying to accomplish. Here is her revised memo:

Dear Supervisors:

To avoid lengthy lineups at the lunch counter, I propose that all departments stagger their lunch hours, starting May 28. I suggest rescheduling the start of your department's lunch hour from noon to 12:30 p.m. Please call me by May 21 if this causes a problem for you.

Carol

Carol's first attempt is informative but not very convincing: it *tells*. Her second attempt tries to get the readers on her side and is more likely to persuade them to accept her proposal: it *sells*.

Decide What the Reader Needs to Know

Knowing how much your reader already knows about the topic provides a starting point for your communications. When Emily Chan wrote to contract employees to inform them that they were to be included in the company pension plan, she was able to start with a direct statement:

The Executive Committee has agreed to extend the company pension plan to all contract employees.

In this case Emily knew that contract employees had already been previously informed that the extension had been proposed, so she wasn't delivering unexpected news. She also knew that other readers, such as permanent employees (who, though not directly addressed, might see her memo), would also not be surprised by the news because the company had also kept them informed of the proposed change, even though it did not affect them.

If the company had worked behind the scenes in preparing this proposal and had not kept the employees informed, Emily's announcement would have come as a surprise. In that case she would have had to build some background information into her memo:

Since its inception in 1994, Vancourt Business Systems' pension plan has applied only to permanent employees. I am pleased to announce that shortly it will also apply to contract employees. The Executive Committee has agreed to extend...

If, like Emily, you know your readers reasonably well, you can easily establish how much they already know about your topic. But if you do not know your readers, or if there are multiple readers, you will need to decide how much information you need to provide. Without doing this preliminary legwork you are likely to have difficulty finding the correct starting point. Understanding who your readers are, what they already know, and what they need to know will help focus your writing and eliminate much of the unnecessary background information that can clutter your memos, letters, reports, and email messages.

Here is a general guideline to help you decide what information you need to include. First, divide your information into two groups:

1. **Need to Know** These are the details that the reader *must* have to fully understand the situation (in a tell message) or to make a decision (in a sell message).

2. **Nice to Know** These are the less important details that *may* interest the reader but are not necessary to fully understand the situation or to make a decision.

Now focus your memo, letter, report, or email message by presenting only the "need to know" details.

An Introduction to the Pyramid Method

Once you have identified who you are writing to and what the purpose of your document is, you need to organize your information in a logical, easy-to-understand order.

Earlier in this chapter we introduced you to the idea of dividing information into two compartments: the Summary Statement and Supporting Details.

The **Summary Statement** tells the reader what he or she most wants to know, or needs to be told, but only in general terms.

The **Supporting Details** compartment provides specific details that support or expand on what has been said in the Summary Statement, this time in concrete terms.

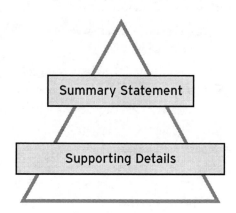

Notice how the information visually forms a pyramid, with the Summary Statement at the top. This reinforces the idea that the Summary Statement should be brief, so it will fit into the small space.

Expanding the Supporting Details

Once you have written the Summary Statement, you need to consider the impact it will have on your readers and anticipate the questions they may have after reading it. What

will they want to know? You can start by asking yourself six basic questions: *What? Who? When? Where? Why?* and *How?* You may not have to answer all six questions, just those that apply to the situation you are writing about. You answer these questions in the Supporting Details compartment.

To help organize the information logically, the Supporting Details compartment is divided into three subcompartments.

Everything you write in these compartments must support or relate to the information you write in the Summary Statement.

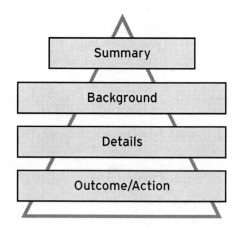

The **Background** compartment sets the scene for the details that follow and answers the questions:

Who *was involved?*

When *did this happen?*

Where did this happen?, and sometimes

Why did this happen?

The **Details** compartment provides all the information the reader needs in order to understand the current status of a project, as in a progress report. This compartment also helps the reader come to a conclusion, make a decision, or give approval, as in a request or proposal. The Details compartment answers the questions:

What has happened, or is happening?

What effect has this had, and *what* has been done about it?

Why did this happen?, and

How did this happen? In some cases explaining "how" may not be necessary–it might be more information than your reader needs to know.

The **Outcome/Action** compartment answers the questions:

What is the result?

What has to be done, by *when*? and by *whom*?

Depending on whether you are writing a tell or a sell document, this last compartment label will vary. For instance, a tell document has an **Outcome** compartment because the last subcompartment only describes *results*, events that have occurred and actions that have already been taken.

A sell document has an **Action** compartment because it identifies who has to act or react (often the reader), and what action that person has to take.

The labels assigned to each compartment are not used as headings in a short memo, letter, or report, although they may appear in a longer document or a formal report.

In the letter to an appliance store manager shown in Figure 1–5, the four writing compartments are clearly defined. Notice how short, direct, and easy to read the letter is when the Pyramid Method is used.

The compartment labels are listed for our purposes only: they would not be present in the letter sent to Mr. Ashe. All Mr. Ashe will know is that the information is presented in a logical, easy-to-understand order and that everything he needs to make a decision is there.

Pyramid Flexibility

The pyramid writing plans presented in this book provide a framework that you can use to organize your information into a coherent document. However, they are not intended to be *rigid* structures that limit your creativity. The number of compartments and their labels can be shaped to suit particular situations. You can use the writing plans as they are, design new ones, or adapt an existing one to suit your specific situation or topic. Simply add, delete, or change the compartments, but always keep in mind who your audience is and what they need to know from you.

Figure 1-5   A letter using the Pyramid Method

Summary
Statement

Background

Details

Action

Dear Mr. Ashe:

The microwave oven we purchased from you has failed for the fourth time in two years. This time I am requesting that you repair it free of charge.

It is the Exalta Model 100B, which we ordered from you on purchase order M2327 dated October 13, 1997, and which you supplied on invoice 13067, dated October 23, 1997. Since then, the microwave oven has had an expensive repair history:

1. The first failure occurred on December 3, 1998, 14 months after the initial purchase and two months after the warranty had expired. Repairs cost $108.00 on your invoice 20016.

2. Five months later, on May 12, 1999, a second breakdown occurred, which cost $87.50 to repair (see invoice 24101).

3. The third failure occurred only three months ago, on August 28, 2000, for which we were billed $126.75 in repair charges on invoice 27833.

To date we have incurred total repair costs of $322.25 – almost half the original purchase price – on a microwave oven which is only three years old. Consequently, I am asking you to pick up the oven by December 2, service it, and return it to us within one week, all at no cost to us.

Regards,

Jonathan Kelly

Jonathan Kelly
Manager

CHAPTER 2

Writing Business Letters, Memos, and Email

It's surprising how much time people spend writing in their everyday work. Electrical engineers have reported that up to 80% of their week is spent communicating. This includes writing letters, memos, email messages, reports, and other forms of documentation. They complain that in college they avoided English classes because they didn't like to write, and now that's all they seem to do!

In Chapter 1 we introduced you to the Pyramid Method of writing and organizing your thoughts and information. Now let's see how the Pyramid Method can be applied to a variety of situations for writing letters, memos, and email. Keep in mind that any of our examples can be used as an email message as well as a letter. The writing is the same regardless of the medium.

Writing Good News and Bad News Letters

Mark is struggling with a letter he needs to write to a client. He is responsible for telling them that their credit application has not been accepted and that the contract work cannot start. He felt the Pyramid Method was too abrupt for sending bad news. Figure 2–1 shows his first attempt, in which he reverted to the climactic way of writing.

Mark felt he should break the news to the Bolands "gently" and decided to start his letter with some pleasantries. Unfortunately, this technique creates the impression that Mark is wishy-washy and afraid of conflict. His writing style doesn't generate confidence. Another potential problem with "hiding" the bad news is that the reader, in this case the Bolands, may only read the first paragraph and think all is well with the project. They may never get to the Summary Statement: "We can't confirm that they will be delivered until your finances are approved."

Figure 2-1   A bad news letter that doesn't use the Pyramid Method

Dear Mr. and Mrs. Boland:

Thank you for submitting your paperwork so promptly to the Genesee Loan Group for review. We are looking forward to working with you in building your house and specifically to installing the kitchen you designed at our offices. I am particularly pleased with your decision to go with the higher quality materials.

As we discussed during our last meeting, I am your contact person at Kreative Kitchens and Design and will be responsible for overseeing all of the work in your new home. The cabinets and countertops have already been ordered and the styles and colours that you requested are available. We had expected delivery to the house within four weeks. Unfortunately, we can't confirm that they will be delivered until your finances are approved.

Mary Jane Dougherty from the Genesee Loan Group has just informed me that your loan application was not approved. This causes a problem with our supplier. Without the proper financing they not only will not deliver the supplies but they also will not guarantee the supplies' availability.

I'm sorry to break this news to you and hope you can resolve this situation soon so we can continue with our original plan; otherwise, the completion date will need to be adjusted.

Sincerely,

Mark

Mark Mathews

Mark's letter would have been clearer and more concise if he had used the Pyramid Method and put a Summary Statement at the beginning. His revised letter is shown in Figure 2–2.

Figure 2-2   A bad news letter using the Pyramid Method

Dear Mr. and Mrs. Boland:

Mary Jane Dougherty from the Genesee Loan Group has just informed me that your loan application was not approved. This causes a problem with our supplier. Without the proper financing they not only will not deliver the supplies but they also will not guarantee the supplies' availability.

As we discussed during our last meeting, I am your contact person at Kreative Kitchens and Design and will be responsible for overseeing all of the work in your new home. The cabinets and countertops have already been ordered and the styles and colours that you requested are currently available. We can expect delivery to the house within four weeks of your financial approval. Unfortunately, we can't confirm that they will be delivered until your finances are approved.

I'm sorry to break this news to you and hope you can resolve this situation soon so we can continue with our original plan; otherwise, the completion date will need to be adjusted. As soon as I receive notice of your finances being approved, I will confirm the order with our supplier.

Sincerely,

Mark

Mark Mathews

In Mark's revised letter, the Bolands immediately understand the problem and what they need to do. They also know what action Mark will take. The letter is shorter, more concise, and creates a confident image of the writer.

Whether you are delivering good or bad news, put the Summary Statement right up front and then follow it with all the Supporting Details.

Types of Letters

Many software packages contain samples and templates of letters you can edit and use. Be careful: it is extremely important that your letters "sound" like you. We want you to develop your own style and know how to organize your thoughts into coherent messages. This section discusses some typical situations and describes the associated writing plans. Remember that the Pyramid Method is flexible, and if you don't see your exact situation here, you can develop your own pyramid using the techniques you are learning.

Writing Complaint Letters

Every day people experience problems with equipment they have purchased and need to explain the situation to the vendor or manufacturer. Other people discover errors in their accounts, such as a payment not having been properly credited, and they need to ask for an adjustment. Sometimes the complaint can be made by telephone or in person, and the matter is resolved quickly. At other times, it is essential to document the situation in writing.

A complaint letter must be firm and definite without sounding abrasive. The person with the complaint must present the facts clearly and definitively, so the reader can readily identify the problem and what action is required. If a complainant shows too much anger or is abusive, he or she may create resistance on the reader's part. See Chapter 6 for information on choosing the right words and avoiding words that might provoke a reader.

Figure 2–3 shows the pyramid for a complaint letter. It breaks the information into four compartments.

1. The **Summary Statement** has two parts:

    a. It identifies what the problem is.

    b. It states the action desired from the reader.

These parts may be combined into a single sentence or broken into two:

Dear Ms. Wahl:

The customized invoice sets you supplied to us on February 15, 2000 were not exactly as ordered, so we are requesting a price reduction.

Figure 2-3 Writing pyramid for a complaint letter

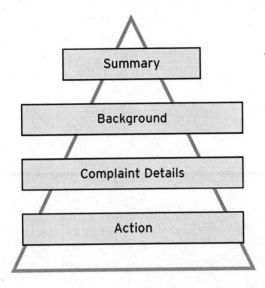

- Very briefly describes the problem and states what action is requested

- Describes the circumstances leading up to the complaint

- Gives specific details of the problem or reason for the complaint

- States exactly what the writer wants the reader to do

The Summary Statement offers generalizations rather than specific details because more exact information will follow later in the letter. Make sure it always contains both the problem *and* a requested action.

2. The **Background** describes the circumstances affecting the complaint and lists the numbers and dates of associated documents:

   They were ordered on our purchase order No. 2463 on January 6 and supplied on your invoice No. 4390 dated February 11.

   In a short letter, the Background compartment can be combined with either the Summary Statement or the Complaint Details compartment to form a single paragraph.

3. The **Complaint Details** compartment describes exactly what is wrong.

   We requested 2000 sets of type 37 invoices imprinted with our company logo, but when the order arrived, we found you sent type 36 invoices in their place.

4. The **Action** compartment identifies what the writer wants the reader to do to correct the problem.

   Rather than destroy the invoices, we have chosen to keep them. We request that you credit our account with the difference between the price of 2000 sets of the type 36 invoice and 2000 sets of the type 37 invoice. We also request an additional 20% discount since we will have to make a duplicate copy of each invoice we raise.

The Action compartment must be absolutely clear, firm, and purposeful. There should be no doubt in the reader's mind what the writer wants done.

The four writing compartments are clearly defined in the letter to a credit card company in Figure 2–4. This is another example of a complaint and a request for adjustment.

Figure 2-4 A request for adjustment

	Dear Customer Accounts Manager:
Summary Statement	There is an error on my July 5 WorldCard statement that has resulted in an overcharge, which I am requesting that you correct.
Background	My WorldCard account number is 312465897; the entry is item 4, dated June 9; the vendor is Burntwood Auto Service; the control number is 0147162; and the amount is $272.40.
Complaint Details	My records for this item show that I bought 51.02 litres of gasoline at 53.4 cents per litre, which calculates to $27.24. This is exactly one-tenth of the amount shown on my statement, which indicates that a decimal point error has occurred.
Action	Please credit my account with $245.16, which is the difference between $27.24 and $272.40, and reverse any interest charges that have been applied.

This is a good example of a situation that cannot be handled over the phone. It needs the follow-up of a written letter so the situation is documented.

Writing a Request Letter

Whether you are requesting funding for new equipment, additional staff, or to attend a conference or course, you need to write your request so that the person who needs to approve it can base their decision on facts that are presented clearly and coherently. Too often people approach the decision maker in person and bombard them with facts and figures. It is unreasonable to expect someone to allocate funding based on a discussion. We suggest you briefly present the request in person (if possible) and then follow your discussion with the details in a concise letter, memo, or email message. Your effort will be appreciated, and will allow the decision maker time to thoroughly review the information. Without time to review all the facts, a decision maker is more likely to deny the request.

Figure 2–5 shows the writing compartments for a request or short proposal letter. They are similar to those for a complaint letter.

1. The **Summary Statement**, which very briefly describes your request and asks for approval.

2. The **Background** or **Reason**, which describes the circumstances leading up to your request, and establishes why the request is important (in very short requests, the Summary Statement and Reason are often combined into a single paragraph).

Figure 2-5 Writing pyramid for a request or short proposal letter

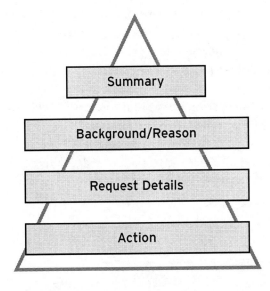

- Very briefly describes the request and asks for approval

- Describes the circumstances and reasons leading up to the request

- Gives specific details of the problem or reason for the request

- States exactly what the writer wants the reader to do

3. The **Request Details**, which describe in detail

- what the request entails,

- what will be gained if the request is granted,

- what problems may be created if the request is approved, and how you plan to overcome or ameliorate them, and

- what the cost will be, financially and to the organization's resources (personnel and material).

4. An **Action Statement**, which identifies clearly what you want the reader to do after he or she has read your request.

The letter in Figure 2–6 shows how a request letter can also be a proposal. Note that in a short letter like this

- the **Summary Statement** and the **Reason** can be in the same paragraph,

- there is both a **Reason** *and* a **Background**,

- the **Background** and **Details** are in the same paragraph, and

- the **Action Statement** states both what the writer wants the reader to do, and what action the writer will take.

This letter demonstrates the flexibility you have when using writing compartments. Whether a single paragraph embraces two compartments or several paragraphs comprise a single compartment is unimportant *providing you keep them in the correct sequence*.

Writing a Reference Letter

You may be asked by someone who has worked for you or with you to write a letter of reference for them. Such letters may be required for employment reasons, to accompany a university or college application, or to gain membership to a professional society.

When someone asks you to write a letter of reference on his or her behalf, try to find out how the letter will be used so that what you write can be tailored to the situation. Whenever possible find out the name of the person to whom your letter will be addressed and sent, or at least the name of the company or organization. This avoids starting the letter with impersonal words like "To Whom it May Concern." Readers understand that these words are bland and non-direct. Letters addressed non-directly are often less credible than those addressed directly to a person. If you don't know who you are writing to, then write to a position:

TO: Human Resources Manager
TO: Potential Employer of Andrew G. Smith
TO: Selection Committee, Simon Fraser University

Figure 2-6 A request or proposal letter

Summary Statement

Reason

Background

Request Details

Action

February 14, 2000

Dear Ms. Yaremko:

I am requesting your approval to change the date of our monthly preventive maintenance service for your Rotomat extruders and shapers to the 29th of each month. This will help spread my technicians' workload more evenly and will provide you with better service.

Our contract with you is No. RE208, dated January 4, 1999, and it requires that we perform monthly inspections and maintenance on the 15th day of each month. Unfortunately, almost all of our clients ask that we perform their maintenance service between the 5th and the 25th, so that we do not overlap the month-end. This creates a problem for us in that our service technicians experience a peak workload for 20 days and then have very little work for 10 days.

Will you please let me know by February 25 if you can accept the change? I will send a technician to your shop on February 29 for a second visit this month, rather than create a six-week space between the February and March inspections. There will be no charge for this extra service.

Sincerely,

Tony

Tony DiCarlo

There are certain facts that a prospective employer or evaluation committee want to hear from you, and they must be built into a fairly short letter. They include, but are not limited to (and not necessarily in this order):

- who you are,
- the connection between you and the person you are writing about,
- the quality of work or service performed by the person you are writing about, and
- special attributes the person has which the *reader* would find valuable.

You should also anticipate the question, "If the opportunity arose, would you rehire this person?" For example, you might write:

If Michele Pierce ever chooses to reapply to us for employment, we would welcome her application.

Figure 2–7 shows the pyramid for a reference letter. It breaks the information into three compartments:

1. The **Summary Statement** identifies the person and briefly comments on his or her main qualities.

2. The **Evidence** compartment supports what is said in the Summary Statement and gives additional information about the person that is useful and relevant. Specific details are particularly important because they increase the credibility of the letter. Writing the sentence

   Janet was employed with us for several years.

   creates a vague or wishy-washy impression. Be specific:

   Janet was employed as a service representative for three years and a traffic superintendent for two years.

   Refer to the person by his or her first name rather than last name (Janet, instead of Ms. Smith), because it will help create the impression that you know the person well and are therefore in a good position to give accurate comments.

3. The **Closing Statement** offers a final comment which can either sum up the person's capabilities or be a more personal statement:

   Janet was a responsible, well-motivated employee. I wish her well in all that she does.

Figure 2-7 Writing pyramid for a reference letter

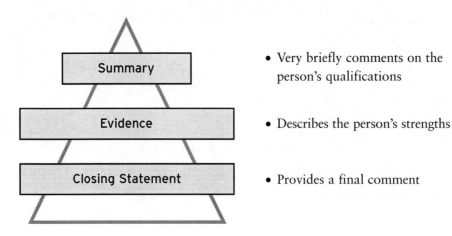

What do you do if you are asked to give a reference for a person who was not a good worker, or was a reasonable worker, but whose interpersonal skills were poor and caused friction among other employees? You can't honestly give a glowing reference, because if the person is hired based on your recommendation and proves to be inadequate, your credibility would be placed in doubt. You have two alternatives:

1. If an individual you are doubtful about asks you for a reference, you can politely decline.

2. If an employer asks you directly for a reference for a person, you can keep it very short and comment briefly on his or her positive aspects, with little or no elaboration.

Figure 2–8 is an example of a reference letter.

Figure 2-8   A reference letter

Dear Potential Employer:

I'm pleased to recommend Matt Jacobs as a qualified and competent pilot to your organization. He possesses both the necessary skills and experience to succeed.

As a Realtor and businesswoman, I was a student of Matt's for six months. I've known him for 18 months. During that time I was able to observe him not only as a flight instructor but also as a member of the community. He is loyal, patient, dependable, flexible, and has excellent judgment.

Through my flight instruction he met my two young boys and always made an extra effort to accommodate their needs. They are both in wheelchairs and Matt's sensitivity and perception were admirable. He still corresponds with the boys. I could always count on Matt to be early to our appointments and he made sure he was there for me in my time frame. He understood and appreciated the time constraints I have with my personal and professional commitments.

I never doubted Matt's abilities or judgment because I always felt secure with him in the plane. More than once he altered the flight pattern and route for safety reasons. For a student, practising safety is an invaluable lesson – for a commercial pilot, it is a requirement. Rarely do you see such confidence in a young man of Matt's age.

In my realty business I meet people with various backgrounds and personalities and I consider myself an excellent judge of character. I have never seen a finer young man than Matt Jacobs and know that whatever he chooses to do in life he will give it 100% and be a success.

Sincerely,

Barbara Johnson

Barbara Johnson

Writing an Instruction Letter

You may have to provide directions to your office staff or client, or explain to a new employee how to access the company's computer system. When providing instructions it is particularly important that your writing is direct, concise, and accurate. The language you use will establish the reader's confidence in both your instructions and their abilities.

Figure 2–9 shows the writing pyramid for an instruction letter. It has four compartments. An Action Statement is unnecessary, because the letter is *informative*.

1. The **Summary Statement** describes very briefly what has to be done.

2. Including a **Reason** is important, because readers more readily follow instructions when they understand why such instructions are necessary. For example, if the instructions explain that the reason for taking a different travel route is to avoid delays, the reader understands why they need to follow the instructions. Frequently, the Reason is stated in the same paragraph as the Summary Statement, and then the **Background** begins a new paragraph.

3. The **Instruction Details** are the steps the reader must follow. Guidelines for writing the steps follow.

   • Keep each step short so the reader does not have to wade through a lengthy paragraph to find out what needs to be done. This also helps the reader remember the details while he or she performs the task.

Figure 2-9 Writing pyramid for an instruction letter

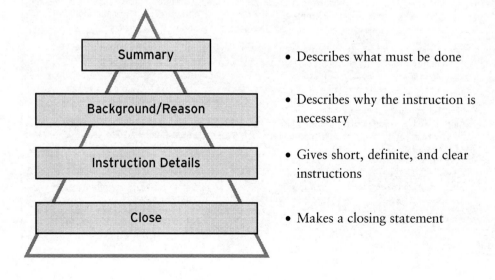

• Describes what must be done

• Describes why the instruction is necessary

• Gives short, definite, and clear instructions

• Makes a closing statement

- Start each step with an active verb, such as *connect, position, calculate,* and *deliver.* Action verbs make your instructions sound authoritative and give readers confidence in you as the instruction giver and in their ability to carry out the task.

- Number each step consecutively if the sequence is essential. Also use numbers if you are showing priority or have to refer back to an item — otherwise, bullets are appropriate.

- Quote specific details rather than generalizations, particularly avoiding ambiguous words such as *about, should, near,* and *close to.*

4. The **Outcome/Action** compartment is often called the Closing Statement because it simply wraps up the memo or letter using positive language.

Figure 2–10 shows an instruction memorandum with a clear and definite tone.

Figure 2-10 An instruction memorandum

Summary Statement and Reason	**To:** Morgan Paulsen **From:** Marita Estavo We have just received a large order that is going to put considerable pressure on the Production Department. Delivery dates are extremely tight, which means you will have to set up the line quickly if the first 100 units are to be shipped on schedule.
Background	The order is for 300 BLS-210 modular interactive learning systems, and the client is Tormont Education Systems Limited (see copy of purchase order, attached).
Instruction Details	Because the first 100 units must be delivered by May 6, we need to complete the following steps: 1. Count the existing stock of system components. 2. Place orders with suppliers *today* for immediate delivery of sufficient additional components to complete the first 100 units. 3. Work out a schedule showing completion dates for parts acquisition, assembly, packing, and shipping. 4. Place follow-up orders with suppliers for delivery of the components for the remaining 200 systems. 5. Inform the system assemblers that they may have to work overtime between April 20 and May 6. 6. Forewarn the shipping department workers that they will need to create 100 designer packing cartons one week in advance of each delivery date.
Closing Statement	I do not foresee any problems in meeting the scheduled deadlines. Call me if you encounter any roadblocks.

Business Letter Format

Many organizations develop a writing style guide that gives employees a set of guidelines for the way their documents should look and the tone and language in which they should be written. Most smaller companies or independent consultants, though, don't have writing guidelines. Because trends change, people are never quite sure of the proper layout for a business letter. Popular word processing packages often include templates for writing business letters, memos, faxes, résumés, proposals, and other documents. Some are very useful; others are distracting and hinder good communication.

The two most common formats for business letters are described here. You may notice some companies are omitting the salutation and complimentary close (e.g. "Dear" and "Sincerely"). We don't encourage this trend, because it makes the letter too impersonal. Also, be aware that as we grow into a more global economy, the European style of writing the date (e.g. day-month-year: 21 September 2000) may become more common. And with the rise of the electronic age, punctuation is often omitted from names and addresses, because it becomes difficult to read online or in a fax. A comma may be mistaken for a period.

Full Block Letter Format

This is the most popular format for business letters today. Notice that in Figure 2–11, every line starts at the left-hand margin. (This is why it is called the full "block" format.) This has evolved over time because it is faster to type. Other features of the full block letter format are outlined below. The numbers correspond to the numbers in Figure 2–11.

① Every line, including the date line, starts flush with the left margin.

② The Post Office asks that the addressee's name appears first, followed by their title and then the name of their company or organization. Sometimes the person's position is placed on the same line as their name and is separated by a comma. You may notice a trend to eliminate all but essential punctuation from the address, greeting, and signature. This will become more prevalent with the use of electronic communication technologies.

③ There should be one blank space between the city and the province or state, and two blank spaces between the province and the postal code (or the state and the zip code), with no punctuation. The province or state is always abbreviated as two capital letters (e.g. "ON" for Ontario).

④ The business trend today is to encourage informality in the greeting by using first names: "Dear Don" instead of "Dear Mr. Lee." You need to be aware of your audience, though, and the reaction that someone who is accustomed to being addressed more formally may have to your greeting. Our guideline is to use the more formal

Figure 2-11 Full block letter format

RGI International
Communication Consultants
4063 South King's Street
Winnipeg MB R3C 3S7
(204) 452 6480

(1) October 16, 2000

(2) Mr. Donald Lee
Chief Executive Officer
Vancourt Business Systems Inc.
2 Sheppard Avenue East
(3) Willowdale ON M2N 5Y7

(4) Dear Don:

My analysis of 300 major companies in Canada and the U.S. shows that 276, or 92%, prefer the full block letter style for their corporate communications and informal letter reports. I have enclosed my report and a graph depicting the industries represented in the survey.

In the full block letter format every line starts at the left margin, which simplifies typing. However, shorter (one-page) letter reports have to be carefully centred vertically on the page if they are to achieve a balanced appearance.

Because it conveys the impression of a modern, forward-thinking organization, I recommend you adopt the full block letter style for Vancourt Business Systems' correspondence.

(4) Sincerely,

Mariah Kaye

(5) Mariah Kaye
Senior Consultant

(6) MK: es

(7) enc: 2

greeting (Dear Mr. Lee) if we are addressing a new client with whom we have never spoken, but to move to first names as soon as we have made contact. Another guideline is to watch how your correspondents sign their letters. The use of a colon (:) after the greeting and a comma (,) after the closing is optional, but make sure you are consistent: if you use a colon following the greeting, then also use a comma following the closing.

⑤ Always type your name and position after your signature; it provides the reader with the correct spelling.

⑥ This is a reference indicating that someone other than the author typed the letter. The capital initials indicate the author and the lower case initials indicate the typist.

⑦ If you enclose or attach other documents to the letter, use this reference to show how many items are included. This is essential, because often the attachments or enclosures are separated from the letter. Some writers list the enclosures (e.g. "report," "graph"). When you enclose or attach materials, make sure you refer to each in the letter.

Modified Block Letter Format

This format is more traditional. Individuals often use this format for their personal correspondence. It's called "modified" because it is based on the full block letter format, with some modifications.

Subject lines are rarely used in modern letters. When you write using the Pyramid Method, they become redundant because your Summary Statement immediately describes what the letter is about. Also, a short, concise letter never needs a subject line. Figure 2–12 shows a letter written in the modified block format.

Some General Letter-Writing Guidelines

Regardless of what letter format you decide to use, there are some general guidelines you should follow.

Balance the Page

A short letter is distracting if it only occupies the top 1/3 of the page. Use some extra spaces between the date and inside address and between the inside address and body to spread the text out over the page.

Double Space Paragraphs

Single space all letters and memos, but to help break up the text, always use an extra line between paragraphs. This will also help balance the page.

Figure 2-12 Modified block letter format

H. L. Winman and Associates
475 Lethbridge Trail
Calgary AB T3M 5G1

November 20, 2000

Andrew Slominski,
Manager, Customer Service
Trident Manufacturing Inc.
6001 Border Road
London ON N6B 3H5

Dear Mr. Slominski:

The modified block letter format is the more conservative and lesser used of the two block letter styles. If you use this format

- type the name and address of the person you are writing flush with the left margin,

- start the line of each paragraph either at the left margin or indented 12 mm, as has been done here,

- start the date and the signature block at the page centerline, and

- ensure that the left and right margins are roughly the same width.

If the report is short enough to fit on one page, position it vertically so that the body of the letter is in the middle of the page.

Sincerely,

Susan Medley

Susan Medley
Publications Editor

Address the Letter to a Person or a Position

If you don't know who you are writing to, either make a quick phone call to find out, or address the letter to the position; for example, "Dear Customer Service Manager" or "Dear RGI Representative." If you address it "To Whom It May Concern," you still need to address the outside of the envelope with a name or position. Otherwise, you risk having your letter end up in the wastepaper basket, because no one knew where to direct it. And, never write "Dear Sir or Madam," because it shows you haven't made an effort to find out to whom your letter should be sent. Besides, most women don't like to be called Madam. If you are responding to a Request for a Proposal and the information is to be sent to M.J. Johnson, and you don't know whether M.J. Johnson is male or female, then simply address the letter "Dear M.J. Johnson."

Use Standard Margins and Fonts

Most readers expect a 1-inch margin on all sides of the text, but to balance the page vertically, you may have to adjust this slightly. Avoid narrowing the margins to make the letter fit onto one page. Choose a pleasing and common font and use an appropriate size. Typically, 10- to 11- point type is readable in most fonts. See "Using Information Design" in Chapter 6 for more information.

Close Professionally

There are only two acceptable closings for professional business letters: "Sincerely" or "Regards." Follow either with your signature and then type your name and position. Avoid using closings such as "Yours Truly," "Warm Regards," and "Yours Faithfully." They are either too formal or too informal, and outdated.

Label Additional Pages

If your letter is longer than one page, label subsequent pages with the reader's name, date, and page number (e.g. "Pierce, p. 2, March 2, 1999"). This helps the recipient if the pages get separated. Use letterhead paper for the first page only.

Internal Memorandum

The memo is the simplest way of reporting information inside an office, but it is slowly being replaced by email. A memo is less formal than a letter, but its paragraphs and sentences still need to be fully developed. Some companies use memo templates — either on a paper form or in a word processing template — which already contain the header fields. Because the addressee's name appears in the "TO:" field, the greeting or salutation is often omitted. The subject line should offer the reader some information about the memo content. For example, if Rick Davis had simply written "Paycheques" as the subject line in Figure 2–13, it would not have been sufficiently informative.

Figure 2-13 An internal memorandum

H. L. Winman and Associates

Internal Memorandum

To: Andy Rittman   From: Rick Davis

Date: December 4, 2000   Subject: Early Mailing of Paycheques
                                           for Field Personnel

I need to know who you will have on field assignments during the week before Christmas so that I can mail their pay cheques early. Please provide me with a list of names, plus their mailing addresses, by December 8.

Cheques will be mailed on Tuesday, December 14. Please inform your field staff of the proposed early mailing.

The "Netiquette" of Electronic Mail

The word "netiquette" has grown only recently into our language. It means, roughly, "the etiquette of writing electronic mail (email) on the net (the Internet)." There are no established guidelines for netiquette, but we can give you some suggestions that will help you be a good email communicator.

Don't forget that email is just one of the communication tools we have available; the telephone and fax machine are more appropriate in many circumstances — and nothing replaces the value of face-to-face communication. Choosing email over a written letter should always be a conscious decision. Remember that just because it is email, it doesn't allow you to

- write snippets of disconnected information,
- write incorrectly constructed sentences,
- forget about using proper punctuation,

- ignore misspelled words, or

- be abrupt or impolite.

Neither, however, is it a forum for telling long stories and anecdotes (you can use regular mail —"snail mail"— for that!).

Many people have the impression that because email is so immediate, the reader will overlook or understand small grammatical or structural errors. These errors, however, create an impression of you and your writing: The "message" you are sending is that you are careless and rushed. Even when using internal email, your readers deserve well-written messages. Remember, too, that it is extremely easy to forward email messages to other people, which means the message you thought you were sending to just one colleague may end up being bounced around to others! Consequently, although misspelled words or poor punctuation might be forgiven by someone in the neighbouring cubicle, your message may be perceived as lacking in quality if it falls into a client's hands or lands on your boss's desk.

Be Careful and Thorough

Proofread email *very* carefully: the informality of the medium and the speed with which you can create and answer messages can invite carelessness. And, unfortunately, most electronic mail providers do not yet have built-in spell checkers.

It may sound contradictory to suggest that you *print* your email messages and edit them on hard copy before you send them, but we recommend that you do so if a message is long or if its contents are particularly important. This is even more necessary if the message is to a customer or client and you are representing not only yourself but also your entire company or organization.

Use the Pyramid Method for Email Messages

You can use the Pyramid Method for writing email messages, just as you do for ordinary letters and reports:

1. Start with what you most want your reader to know and, if appropriate, what action you want the reader to take. Because of the limited viewing space on computer screens, it is even more important to put your Summary Statement at the beginning.

2. Follow with any Supporting Details the reader may need to understand the reason for your message, and provide information about any point that may need further explanation.

Check that each message contains *only* the information your reader will need to respond or to act — and no more. That is, take care to separate the essential *need to know* information from the less important *nice to know* details.

Be Professional and Ethical

Remember that email is not a good medium for conveying confidential information, and is especially not a good medium for making uncomplimentary remarks about other people. Email messages can too easily be forwarded or copied to other readers, and then you have no control over who else might see what you have written. Be as professional in writing email messages as you are in writing regular letters and memos.

Similarly, be just as sensitive when deciding to copy a message to another person. Be sure in your mind that the original sender would want his or her message distributed to a wider audience.

"Emoticons" are icons or pictures that show emotion when you look at the symbols sideways. For example, :-) is a smiling face and :-(is a frowning face. There are hundreds of these emoticons. However cute they may seem, they are not professional and do not belong in business email messages. Some people may not understand what they are or may consider you to be immature if you use them.

Some Additional Guidelines

Here are some suggestions that will help you write more effective email messages:

- Remember that busy readers who receive many messages want them to be concise, yet complete. Feed the needs of such readers and eliminate unnecessary information.

- If you are writing to multiple readers, consider sending *two* messages rather than a single, all-embracing one. Write

    1. a short summary, which you send to readers who are interested only in the main event and the result, and

    2. a detailed message, which you send to readers who need all the details.

- Be selective when replying to a multiple-reader message. It may be tempting to simply click the "Reply All" button rather than take the time to address your reply to only those readers who need it. Remember that if you click the "Reply All" button, your message will go to everyone on the original list. If other people reply to messages in the same way, the network system — and everyone's In Basket — will quickly become overloaded.

- When accessing email, download it to your computer and into your In Basket so that your messages do not remain on the server, taking up extra space. You would be surprised how fast valuable server space is eaten up by email messages. Learn how to read and write messages offline (i.e. without being connected to the server) so you don't tie up telephone lines or network connections.

- Avoid letting messages accumulate for too long in your In Basket. If you want to keep a message or refer to a message later, store it in an electronic "project folder" in the "filing cabinet" (or electronic receptacles with similar names, depending on the software you are using). Make sure you periodically review what you have filed in folders, otherwise you'll become an electronic "pack rat." There are many messages, like old meeting agendas, that you may store electronically, but would never dream of storing on paper.

- Avoid routinely printing copies of messages you want to keep: creating extra paper defeats the goal of email!

- Use the subject line to identify the content of your message. Make it relevant and meaningful. Subjects like "Forwarded Message," "Question," or "None" don't encourage the reader to open the message and read it. Some people will look at the sender names in their In Basket to decide which messages need attention first.

- When replying to a message, particularly if your reply will go to multiple addressees, quote a line or two from the original message to help put your reply into context. Identify the excerpt by placing a ">" sign before each line, like this:

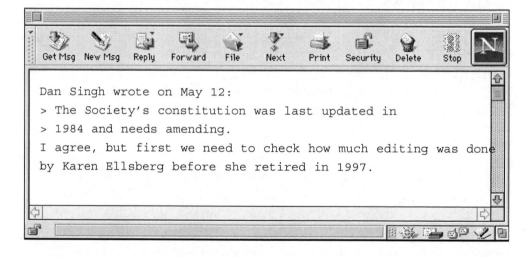

Some email systems will automatically identify original text in a reply, and in others, you may have to type it in yourself. Learn how your particular system works.

- Write your name at the bottom of every message you create, even though your name appears in the "To-From" list at the top. If a recipient decides to forward the message to other people, frequently, only the text will be forwarded and then recipients will not be able to identify the originator. Without your name (or a signature file), it might create the impression that you don't have time or you don't think the reader needs your name attached to the message. When we receive messages without the author's name we feel like we do when we get unsolicited, generic, junk mail with a stamped signature on the bottom.

- If you are annoyed or irritated by a message you receive, *wait* before replying so you won't regret sending a message written in the haste of an emotional moment. Let your irritation cool down. Email is ideal for transmitting facts, but is the wrong medium for sending emotionally charged messages.

- Use only simple formatting. Write short paragraphs with line lengths of no more than 60 characters, and separate each paragraph with a blank line. Avoid creating columns and indenting subparagraphs, because what you see on screen most likely will not be what your reader sees. For example, your screen may look like this:

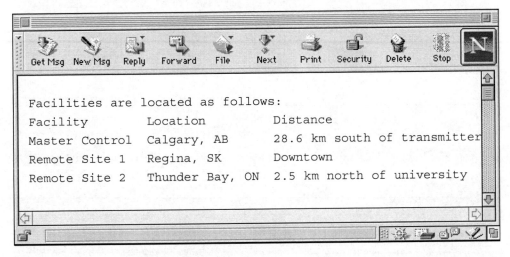

But your reader may see something like this:

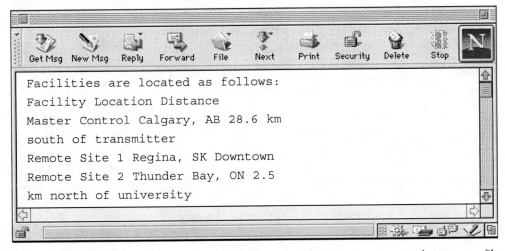

If you need to format columns, consider creating the message as a word processor file and sending it as an attachment to an email message. (This can be done well with some programs, less effectively with others.) Use attached files only for longer messages or reports. With some computer systems, the process of receiving and opening attached files can take two to three times longer than receiving a simple email message. You also need to make sure the reader's system can accept your word processor file format.

- With most email software you cannot use boldface or italic type in a message. If you want to emphasize a word, insert an asterisk on both sides of the word or expression:

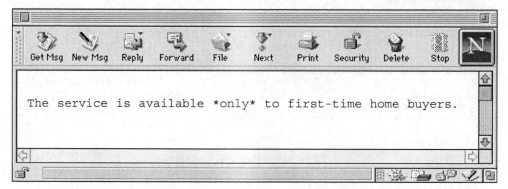

- Avoid bellowing! Use upper and lower case letters, particularly for headings, just as we have done throughout this book. Never present messages in uppercase letters:

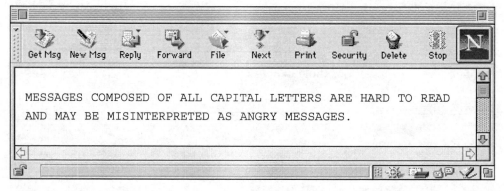

- Avoid whispering!

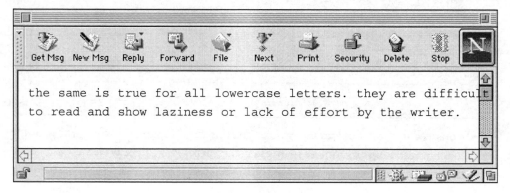

CHAPTER 3

Writing Short Reports

Why Write Reports?

Managers in a well-run company need to be fed a continual stream of information about what is happening in their departments. This does not mean a manager's role is simply to act as a watchdog, keeping an eye on every employee and checking that everyone is doing their job properly. Rather, it means that each manager needs to know what is being done for each task, what problems have been experienced, how the problems have affected work progress, and whether the problems will cause a delay in a particular project's planned completion date. Managers use this information to plan future work, to assign additional staff to a task, to predict operating costs, to develop a budget for future activities, and to report profitability to the company's executives.

As a report writer, the information that you provide can vary. For example, you might have to describe the results of a meeting you held with a client, or a power outage that stopped production on an assembly line and ruined a set of tests you were conducting, or what progress has been made on a software program you are developing for one of the company's customers.

You may pass some of this information on to your supervisor by word of mouth, present a report as an activity update to a group of people at a department meeting, or prepare a short written report to your immediate peers. In each case your report would appear as a memo, letter, fax, or email, and its shape should evolve from the writing pyramids described in Chapter 2. Chapters 3 and 4 show how the writing compartments can be expanded and reshaped to suit each situation and the information you have to convey.

Types of Short Reports

A hospital nurse working the night shift has to leave a note for the ward supervisor (who works the day shift) to inform her that the respirator was knocked over during the night and must be sent out for repair. A designer has to describe to an architect how his CAD designs are progressing. A sales executive needs to explain what happened during a meeting at a client site. A plumber installing toilets in a new high-rise apartment block has to inform the building contractor that the holes cut in the eighth floor of a new apartment building are too small to accept the pipe chosen for the job, that she has spent extra time enlarging the holes, and that she will have to charge for the extra work she has done. A project manager has to explain the lessons learned during the 13-month development cycle of new processing equipment.

All five have a message to **tell**:

- The nurse has to *tell* the ward supervisor....
- The designer has to *describe* progress to the architect....
- The sales executive has to *explain* to the management team....
- The plumber needs to *inform* the contractor....
- The project manager has to *explain* to other project managers....

Each of these reports deals with facts. Their writers have to *tell* their readers about something that has happened or is currently happening. There are five types of reports:

1. To report an event or accident,

   you write an **incident report**. (The nurse.)

2. To report what was done during a field assignment (on a job that was done away from your regular place of work),

   you write a **field assignment report** or, simply, a **field report**. (The sales executive.)

3. To report on the condition of a location, building, or equipment,

   you write an **inspection report**. (The plumber.)

4. To describe how a job is progressing (for a project that is not yet complete),

   you write a **progress report**. (The designer.)

5. To describe a job or task that is finished,

   you write a **project completion report**. (The project manager.)

All five types of reports are described in this chapter.

Sometimes, however, you may have to describe what you have seen or heard and, if you have been reporting a problem or describing a difficult situation, suggest what should be done to correct or improve it. When this occurs,

you write an **investigation report** or an **evaluation report**.

These are longer reports that tell what has happened and *sell* (i.e. persuade) their readers to approve the action you recommend should be taken. They are described in Chapter 4.

Reporting an Event or Incident

An incident report uses the same pyramid structure we suggested you use for letters and memos in Chapter 2. Figure 3–1 shows it has the same four-compartment writing plan. Only one label changes:

1. The **Summary Statement** briefly describes the incident and its main effects.

2. The **Background** section describes the circumstances leading up to the incident. It describes who was involved and when and where the incident occurred.

3. The **Event** covers the incident (i.e. what happened), but in much more detail than in the Summary Statement.

4. The **Outcome** identifies factors evolving from the event, discusses their implications, and describes what action you have taken as a result of the incident.

The length of an incident report can vary from being very short to moderately long, depending partly on the size and effect of the Event, and partly on the amount of information the reader needs to fully understand the Event and its effects. It can be as simple as a single sentence:

On May 27, in our Regent Avenue plant, a fire caused a one-day loss of production.

Here, the **Background** is:

On May 27, in our Regent Avenue plant,...

Figure 3-1   Writing pyramid for an incident report

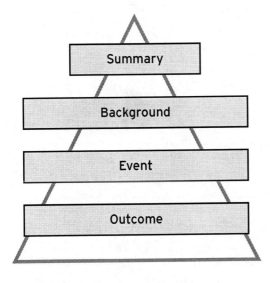

- Briefly describes what happened and the impact

- Describes the circumstances leading up to the event

- Describes in detail what happened

- States the result

The **Event** is:

a fire...

And the **Result** is:

caused a one-day loss of production.

For most readers such a basic statement would be inadequate. If you were a company executive, you would expect a much more detailed report: one similar to that in Figure 3–2.

Figure 3-2   An incident report using the Pyramid Method

INTER-OFFICE MEMORANDUM

To: Vern Rampersaad, Vice President

From: Sheena Walters, Personnel Supervisor

Date: January 21, 2000

Ref: Work stoppage at Regent Avenue

Summary
Statement

A fire has caused a one-day loss of production at our Regent Avenue plant.

Background

The incident occurred at 8:45 a.m. on Monday, January 20, 2000. The fire started in the kitchen of The Stepp Inn cafe, which is housed in the same building and is immediately adjacent to our assembly line test station.

Event

The fire was caused when the handle on a pail of cooking oil broke as the pail was being lifted onto the stove. The oil spilled onto the burners and ignited immediately.

When the fire department arrived at 8:57 a.m., the fire chief ordered a complete evacuation of the building. The fire was extinguished by 10:30 a.m.

The fire completely gutted The Stepp Inn and burned a 1.30 m diameter hole through the wall separating the cafe from our offices. Our assembly line test station received considerable smoke and water damage. Because of the smoke and fumes that permeated the building, the fire chief did not permit staff to re-enter the building until 6:15 p.m.

Outcome

I have instructed ARC Builders Ltd. to install a temporary wall at the east end of the building, in front of the fire-damaged wall. The temporary wall will be completed overnight. I have also rented air extractors to remove fumes.

The work stoppage will put us one day behind schedule with our contract to assemble modules for the Krypton Corporation.

In a very short report, a single paragraph may cover more than one compartment. For instance, the following paragraph covers both the **Summary Statement** and the **Background**:

> **The May 19 inspection of microwave tower No. 14 shows that the transmission line on the vertical riser is frayed and needs to be replaced.**

In a long incident report, each writing compartment may contain several paragraphs (as the **Event** compartment does in Figure 3–2). When a report is long, it's a good idea to introduce each writing compartment with a heading. Although you could use **Background**, **Event**, and **Outcome** as headings, try to create headings that better represent the content. For the fire damage report in Figure 3–2, for example,

To introduce	You could use this heading
The Background	Location of Fire
The Event	Extent of Fire
The Outcome	Post-fire Action

Reporting a Field Assignment

Whenever you return from a field assignment, you will be expected to write a brief report describing what you saw, what you did, and, sometimes, what still needs to be done. (A field assignment is a job done away from your normal place of work.) This applies just as much to a one-hour visit to a local computer distributor to see a new software program demonstrated, as it does to a three-week stay at a paper mill during which you and two other team members replace old wiring and install a new control panel. The report you write should describe your impressions (of the computer software) or provide a detailed account of the work that was done (at the paper mill). You should submit a written report rather than a spoken report partly because you shouldn't trust your memory to remember details several months after the assignment. A written report is essential mostly because your company will need a permanent record of what was done and to help technicians who visit the site and work with the same equipment or people in the future.

The four writing compartments for a field assignment report are shown in Figure 3–3.

Figure 3-3   Writing pyramid for a field assignment report

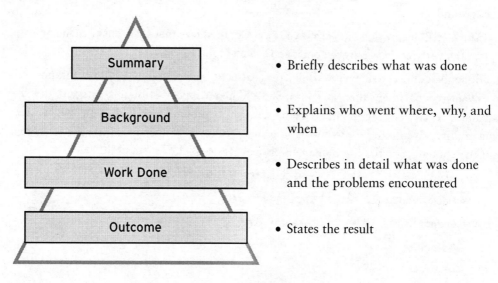

- Briefly describes what was done

- Explains who went where, why, and when

- Describes in detail what was done and the problems encountered

- States the result

1. In the **Summary Statement**, *briefly* describe where you went and what you did or achieved, and comment on the trip's outcome.

2. In the **Background**, provide information about the assignment that is not a *doing* part of the job. Generally, this means answering the questions: *Who* went *where*, *when*, and *why*? For example:

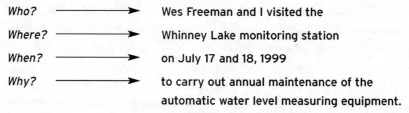

You may also include information such as the name of the person authorizing the trip, the type of transportation you used (e.g. personal or company automobile, scheduled airline flight, or charter helicopter), and the names of people you worked with or contacted at the job site.

In a very short trip report you may combine the Background with the Summary Statement.

3. In the **Work Done** compartment, describe what you did while at the job site or on the field assignment. This can range from a short description of a routine test of a radio transmitter and receiver, to a long narrative pointing out problems with the transmitter and describing unscheduled work you had to carry out to make it work at top operating potential.

In a longer report, we suggest you break this compartment into three sub-compartments:

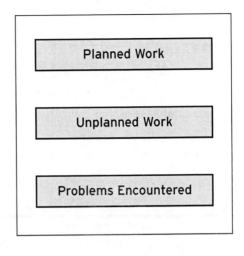

a)   Write about **Planned Work** or routine work very briefly. If possible, refer to an instruction sheet or maintenance procedure rather than mentioning all the details of the work that was done.

b)   Cover unusual or **Unplanned Work** in more detail, because it will be new to the reader. State what you did, why you did it that way, and what the results were.

c)   Explain the **Problems Encountered** in detail, so readers understand the factors that made the job more difficult than expected and, if necessary, what steps should be taken to prevent the problems from happening again.

4.   In the **Outcome** compartment, comment on the main achievement(s) or result(s) of your visit and draw attention to any work that you could not do or finish. If possible, suggest how, when, and by whom the work should be done or completed.
     A short informal trip report is shown in Figure 3–4.

Figure 3-4   A short field assignment report

Summary
Statement
and Background

Hilary:

My examination of the Rega model 301 bread-slicing machine shows it would be a good choice for our bakery. I examined the 301 in operation on October 20 at Modern Bakeries' Main Street plant, at the invitation of MB's production assistant, George Fenton.

Work Done

The Rega 301 is fast, efficient, and extremely safe. It fully lives up to the manufacturer's claims in the attached advertising leaflet. Mr. Fenton said that it regularly slices 2700 loaves per hour, which is 20% faster than our machine. They have two Rega 301s and have had no breakdowns in the seven months they have been in operation. The 301's positive safety features are particularly attractive.

Outcome

I am convinced this is the right machine for our bakery and recommend we budget $16 000 to buy three next year.

Nancy

Reporting Course or Conference Attendance

You can use the field assignment writing pyramid to describe the results of a course or conference you have attended by changing the **Work Done** compartment to **Course/Conference Details**. Figure 3–5 shows the four writing compartments.

1. In the **Summary Statement**, state what course or conference you attended and the main impact it had on you. For example:

   > TO: Vince Warchuk, Manager Human Resources Department
   >
   > The *Making Effective Oral Presentations* seminar I attended presented useful information and provided ample opportunities for practice. I suggest we bring the seminar in-house for other supervisors.

2. In the **Background** answer the questions *Who? When? Where? Why?*:

   > The seminar was presented by Joan Porter-Farr of Presentations International, Toronto. It was held at the Norfolk Hotel from 9 a.m. to 4:30 p.m. and the cost was $235 per person. There were 12 participants, which is the maximum recommended to ensure individual attention for each participant.

3. In the **Course/Conference Details** compartment, identify the topics you want to discuss. We suggest choosing topics from the following list:

   - Identify your expectations or objective(s) in attending the course or conference.

Figure 3-5   Writing pyramid for course or conference attendance

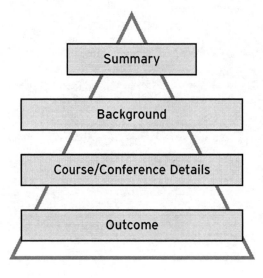

- Briefly describes the course or conference and its value to the writer

- Describes who went where, why, and when

- Provides a detailed description of the course or conference

- States the result and possible follow-up

- Describe your overall reaction to the course or conference and whether your expectations or objective(s) were met.

- Describe the course: state how it was presented and what you did.

- Mention what aspect of the course or conference was of particular value to you.

- Comment on the quality of the course or conference, covering

  ♦ the effectiveness of the presenters or instructors,

  ♦ the pacing (particularly for a course or seminar),

  ♦ the visual aids and handout materials, and

  ♦ the facilities.

Here is an example (continuing from the earlier scenario):

My objective was to increase my confidence when making oral presentations to clients and to in-house staff. I was also asked to evaluate the suitability of the seminar for other company employees. My objectives were fully met: practising both planned and impromptu speaking has given me much greater confidence in preparing a presentation and responding to listeners' questions.

The seminar was divided into three sessions:

1. During the first two hours the seminar leader described informal and semiformal speaking techniques. She stressed the need for speakers to repeat an idea three times: start with an introductory summary, then provide the full details, and end with a conclusion that sums up the main points.

2. In the second half of the morning, the participants interviewed each other and presented a two-minute personal description. This was followed by impromptu two-minute presentations of a topic defined by the seminar leader.

3. The afternoon was devoted to practical speaking exercises, during which each participant presented a three-minute and a six-minute talk. I found this to be the most useful part of the seminar.

   The seminar was very well presented. Ms. Porter-Farr established an informal setting that helped relax the participants. Yet she kept the seminar fast-paced and businesslike. There were 30 pages of handout notes that summarized the key points and provided exercises for future practice (see attached). The room at the Norfolk Hotel was a good size, but has acoustic problems: occasionally we could hear laughter and applause from the presentation in the next room.

4. In the **Outcome** or **Action** statement, sum up with an overall comment about the effectiveness of the course or conference and, if appropriate, include a recommendation:

The *Making Effective Oral Presentations* seminar provides a valuable learning experience. I recommend we either enroll staff to attend the next open-registration seminar (planned for January 27) or ask Ms. Porter-Farr to bring the seminar in-house. I enclose a cost sheet for both scenarios.

Marge Watson

Reporting an Inspection

People who are particularly good at their work sometimes are promoted to the position of inspector, so they can check on work done by others. In the building trades, for example, a skilled craftsperson may check on work being done at several small construction sites or act as the resident inspector on a large construction project.

The reports inspectors write are called inspection reports, and are actually extended field assignment reports. They follow the five-compartment writing pyramid shown in Figure 3–6.

1. The **Summary Statement** describes, in just a few words, the general condition you found or the overall impression you gained during your inspection. For example:

   Installation of the data processing equipment is on schedule, but minor deficiencies may prevent switchover on the planned date.

Figure 3-6 Writing pyramid for an inspection report

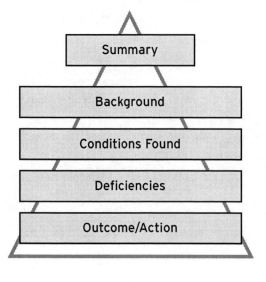

- Briefly describes what was observed, and the result of the inspection

- Describes who went where, why, and when

- Describes the quality and/or quantity of the work or site inspected

- Describes what needs to be corrected

- States the overall result and gives a recommendation

2. The **Background** describes the circumstances relating to the inspection. Like a field assignment report, it answers the question: *Who* went *where, why,* and *when?*:

> My visit to the Boris Lake site took place on September 13. It was authorized by Dave Jarvis who, in a September 8 memo, asked me to check on installation status.

3. Under **Conditions Found** you describe what you observed during the inspection. If you are assessing the *quantity* of work done, these could be the

   - *cubic metres* of concrete poured,
   - *number* of doors hung,
   - *extent* of painting completed,
   - *depth* of excavation reached,
   - *length* of cable installed,
   - *percentage* of piles sunk, and so on.

   However, if you are assessing the *quality* of work done, you would comment on the condition of the work that has been done. For instance:

   > The wallpaper has been raggedly trimmed and has air bubbles under it.

   Or

   > The *4Tell* software program has a bug that prevents the user from saving his or her work.

   If you are commenting on both quantity *and* quality, you can broaden your description like this:

   > Drape tracks have been installed in all rooms of the main floor, but the work has been poorly done. The track in room A3 is not properly centred, and the track in room A6 slopes downward from right to left.

4. **Deficiencies** are all the things you feel must be corrected; that is, work that has not been done or has been poorly done. List each deficiency as a separate item, give it a number, and use strong, definite words to indicate that the work *must* be done or the item *must* be repaired (i.e. use strong expressions such as *is to, will,* and *must*, but not a weak word such as *should*). Here are two examples:

   Weakly worded deficiencies:

   1. The drape track over window 4 in room A6 should be realigned so that it appears horizontal.

   2. The green and yellow wires to pin B of terminal 17 should be resoldered.

More strongly worded deficiencies:

1. The drape track over window 4 in room A6 must be realigned so that it is horizontal.

2. The green and yellow wires to pin B of terminal 17 are to be resoldered.

An even better and more affirmative way to list deficiencies is to put a strong verb at the start of each deficiency, such as *Replace, Reinstall, Insert,* or *Connect.* This turns your deficiency into a definite instruction:

Two even more-strongly worded deficiencies:

3. *Realign* the drape track over window 4 in room A6 so that it is horizontal.

4. *Resolder* the connections between the green and yellow wires and pin B of terminal 17.

It's important to keep the conditions found and the deficiencies as two separate compartments within your report. If you state each deficiency immediately after describing the condition you observed, you will create a series of statements like this:

5. On microwave tower 5, in several places the space between cable lacings exceeds the maximum specified in directive EL283, para. 61. Additional lacing must be installed so the maximum spacing between lacings is no more than 0.90 m.

The result is a series of subparagraphs that are coherent in themselves, but in which a reader will have difficulty quickly identifying what corrective action needs to be taken. By keeping them as separate compartments, your readers will be able to find the deficiencies easily and know that the list is complete.

An alternative way to list conditions and deficiencies is to create a table. The example in Figure 3–7 changes the title *Deficiency* to *Corrective Action.* This informs the reader specifically what has to be done.

Note that Conditions Found can be general statements, but Corrective Action *must* state specifically what has to be done.

5. The **Outcome/Action** compartment has a dual purpose:

    • To make a final comment about the site or project being inspected.

    • To make a recommendation if further action needs to be taken.

For example:

Although the computer and integrated software have been properly installed, the system will not be fully operational until operator training is complete. The training will be finished by May 10. If an earlier start-up date is necessary, I recommend that two operators be flown to Toronto for training by Hazelton Systems Ltd.

Figure 3-7 An inspection report prepared as a table

Conditions Found	Corrective Action
1. Processor-controllers: 15 are operational, 2 are unserviceable.	1. Repair or replace processor controllers 4A and 7B.
2. Tranmission by fibre optic cable to the remote site is satisfactory.	——
3. Two of the video monitors are Nabuchi model 100. The remainder are model 200.	3. Raise a requisition to replace older model 100 video monitors with new Nabuchi model 200.

Some employers use printed forms, like the one in Figure 3–8, for their inspectors to complete when writing their inspection reports. This considerably simplifies the inspectors' writing, because it automatically divides the information into writing compartments.

In Figure 3–8 the Background information is included in the first section. It is labelled Inspection Details and precedes the Summary Statement (here called the Inspection Summary).

Reporting Progress

When you are working on a project for an extended length of time, you will occasionally be asked to write a progress report for your supervisor or manager. Your report should answer three questions:

1. How is the job progressing?

2. Have you run into any problems and, if so, what have you done about them?

3. When will you complete the job and, if you are behind schedule, what action are you taking to try to finish on time?

The simplest way to present this information is in a logical sequence from the past, through the present, to the future. So, once again, you have a five-compartment writing pyramid, as shown in Figure 3–9.

Figure 3-8   An inspection report written on a prepared form

Inspection Report

Inspection Details

Location: 521 Barclay Bay   **Date:**   August 29, 2000

Item(s) Being Inspected: Interior Decorating

Inspector: Ray Dryfuss   **Contractor:**   Phil-Dec Limited

Inspection Summary

Progress and workmanship are generally good, although some deficiencies need to be corrected.

Conditions Found

- The carpet for the living room and front hall has not been installed. The carpet has been received, but the underpad has not been delivered.
- All walls and ceilings have been painted and are satisfactory.
- All wallpaper has been hung. The work is satisfactory in the kitchen and bathroom, but not in the dining room.
- Trim around the doors and windows has been installed and is satisfactory.
- Tiles have been installed in the bathroom and kitchen: satisfactory.
- The rubber baseboard has been poorly installed in the bathroom and kitchen.

Deficiencies

1. Install carpet and underpad in the living room and front hall.
2. Strip and rehang wallpaper in the dining room.
3. Clean up the mess around the baseboard in the kitchen and bathroom. Install new baseboard where the previously installed baseboard does not fit properly.

Recommendations

1. Because of the delay in delivery of the underpad, I recommend that the contractor's invoice be paid (less $700) as soon as deficiencies 2 and 3 have been corrected.
2. Re-inspect the property when all deficiencies have been corrected.

Figure 3-9   Writing pyramid for a progress report

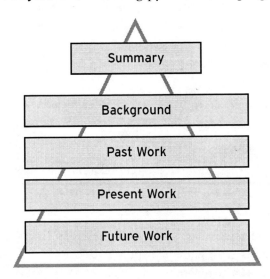

- Briefly describes status of project

- Describes the circumstances, including project history

- Describes work done, plus problems encountered

- Describes what is being done now

- States what is planned, and comments on the schedule

1. The **Summary Statement** is a particularly important feature of progress reports. Managers are especially interested in whether each project is on schedule, so tell them right away what they most want to know. Here is an example, written by Candace to her project manager:

   Although work at the construction site is two days behind schedule, I expect the crew to finish the job on May 18, the planned completion date.

   Now that Candace has told her manager the project is behind schedule (but has immediately set her manager's mind at ease), she'll explain in the rest of the report how she arrived at this general statement.

2. In the **Background** compartment Candace describes factors affecting the job, such as project authorization details, contract number and date, who is involved in doing the work, and the project start and expected completion dates.

3. In **Past Work**, Candace describes work she has done to date. If she had written a previous report, she can divide the Past Work into two segments:

   1. A general part, in which she tells what has been done since the job started.

   2. A more detailed part, in which she describes what has been done since the previous report was written.

   The length and depth of topic coverage depends on the particular situation. If only a general statement of progress is necessary and the project has been running smoothly, then keep the Past Work entry short. For example:

   Since arriving at the Port Coquitlam property on October 17, we have rebuilt the interiors of all six rooms and have painted two of them.

However, if the reader will want more exact information, or if there is a problem or unusual situation to report, then you will have to insert more details. These should include *facts,* such as the quantity of items completed, the number of hours worked, or the amount of materials used. If there is an extensive list, attach it as a separate sheet and refer to it in the report.

4. In **Present Work**, Candace describes what is currently being done. This may be no more than a short paragraph or even a single sentence:

We are now cutting and installing indoor-outdoor carpet.

It can also describe what is being done to bring a delayed project back onto schedule:

The crew is working two hours overtime three evenings this week to recover 18 hours of lost time.

5. In **Future Work**, Candace tells the reader what she plans to do next and, if the project is behind schedule, forecasts a revised final completion date. If the job is running smoothly it can usually be a short statement:

The siding and shingles will be started on Monday so that, weather permitting, we will finish the job on Friday May 18.

But if there are problems and the project is behind schedule, Candace must tell her reader what her plans are and how she intends to put them into effect:

I plan to wire up the main control panel this week so the government inspector can check the building on May 13. I will then finish installing the control unit in room A301 and do the site operational test on May 16, two days behind schedule.

Figure 3–10 shows an example of a short progress report.

Reporting Project Completion

When you finish a project or task, you will be expected to write a report that documents key features about the work you did and whether any work is outstanding. In one sense, a project completion report is like a final progress report in that it has a five-compartment writing pyramid (see Figure 3–11).

The writing compartments for a project completion report should contain the following information:

1. The **Summary Statement** identifies that the project is complete and states whether there is any special information the reader needs to know.

2. The **Background** is similar to that of a progress report: it states who authorized the project, its starting date and planned completion date, and who was involved.

Figure 3-10 A short progress report

MEMORANDUM

To: Kelly Freeland

From: Glen Marguson

Date: August 15, 2000

Subject: Progress: lunchroom modernization

Summary Statement

At the midpoint of the lunchroom modernization project the contractor is roughly on schedule. We can expect to start using the lunchroom again on September 8, as planned.

Background

During the first three weeks the contractor (Jorgensen Construction Company of Guelph, Ontario) has completed all major construction work, installed new plumbing and wiring, and started the painting and decorating.

Past Work

He had to leave a space for the steam table, which will not be delivered until September 6, but says it can be installed in one day without disturbing other equipment. Currently he is building the lunch counter, storage cabinets, buffet, and serving area.

Present Work

Future Work

The contractor estimates all construction, decorating, and major installation work will be completed by August 31. This will leave one week for the kitchen supplier to install and hook up the serving area equipment, which is scheduled to take only 2.5 days. The steam table will be installed and hooked up on September 7.

Kelly

3. The **Project Highlights** compartment describes the most important aspects of the project and what was achieved.

4. The **Exceptions** compartment identifies any variances from the original project plan and discusses why the variances were necessary, how they affected the project, what actions were taken because of the variance, and whether any further action is necessary. For example:

Figure 3-11 Writing pyramid for a project completion report

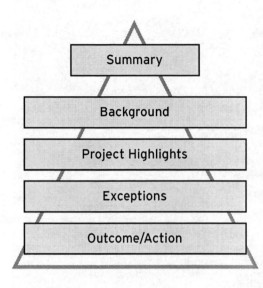

- States that the project is complete and describes the main outcome

- Describes the project's purpose and overall objectives

- Describes key milestones and objectives reached

- Describes variances from original project plan

- States overall result; includes a recommendation

At site 17, we were unable to install the AV61 sensor in the location specified by installation instruction SC28, para. 28.2. A humidity control box had already been installed in that location, so we constructed a 290-mm-wide x 210-mm-deep shelf to the left of the humidity control box and mounted the sensor on it. This called for additional cabling to connect the sensor to the master control station. A drawing of the installation is included in attachment 3.

5. The final compartment is called either **Outcome** or **Action**:

    - It is an **Outcome** compartment if the project is complete and no further work needs to be done or no further decisions need to be made. In such cases the Outcome may be no more than a single sentence stating that the project is complete.

    - It is an **Action** compartment if further work is necessary. The Action compartment lists what has to be done, and when and by whom it should be done. Here is an example:

    I will arrange for a replacement standby power pack to be shipped to site 17, where I have left installation instructions with the resident technician. The power pack will be shipped on June 12 and installed by June 15.

Figure 3–12 shows a typical project completion report.

Figure 3-12 A project completion report

MEMORANDUM

To: Elizabeth Watson

From: Sandy Carstairs

Date: January 28, 2000

Subject: Evaluation: End-use of Model Nabuchi 280A PCs

Summary
Statement

My examination of customer purchase orders for the Nabuchi Model 280A portable computer shows that we are entitled to a refund of $35 957.04 from Revenue Canada for duty paid on imported components.

Background

The 3000 model 280A PCs we manufactured between May 1998 and October 1999 each contained a disk drive that we bought from Nabuchi Industries in South Korea. We paid an import duty of $28.56 for each drive. A November 15, 1999 ruling by Revenue Canada now permits imported components installed in products delivered to educational institutions to be brought into Canada duty-free. This ruling was subsequently made retroactive to January 1, 1998, which encompasses the entire production run for the Model 280A.

Project
Highlights

Our inventory shows that 2882 of the 3000 280A PCs we manufactured have been sold. My research into customer purchase orders and our invoices has identified 1259 units that were bought by educational institutions. This means we can claim a $28.56 refund on the 1259 units, for a total refund of $35 957.04.

Exceptions

There were 84 units for which I was unable to identify an end use: 7 were purchased by customers who have since declared bankruptcy, 2 were destroyed in fires, 13 were stolen and not recovered, 34 were resold and therefore ineligible for a refund, and 28 could not be traced.

Outcome

I will prepare a claim letter to Revenue Canada for your signature and, for the remaining 118 unsold units, I will keep a running record of purchases and declared end use.

Sandy

CHAPTER 4

Writing Longer Reports

Semiformal reports can vary in length from two or three pages to 30 or more, and may be issued either in letter form or presented more formally with a printed title page stapled to the front. Reports may cover a variety of subjects that usually fall into three main categories:

1. An **investigation** to resolve a problem or improve an unsatisfactory condition.

2. An **evaluation** of a system or operating procedure.

3. A **comparative analysis** of alternative methods or techniques.

A general writing pyramid can be used with only minor modifications for all three categories.

Reporting an Investigation

An investigation is carried out whenever there is a need to look into a problem or to find a better way of doing something. The range of topics can vary widely. For example, you might

- evaluate several compact minivan models to assess which would be the best replacement for the company's three aging full-size vans,

- consider better ways to store and issue spare parts,

- investigate why there has been a big increase in the number of poorly machined parts coming from your department,

- look for a better way to pack oval products into shipping cartons, or

- investigate how rainwater has been seeping into a storage area.

At the end of your investigation you will need to describe what you have discovered and recommend what needs to be done. You may present your findings orally, or as a written report prepared in one of three ways:

1. As a memorandum addressed to someone in the company (usually your department head).

2. In a letter on company letterhead addressed to someone outside the company (often, a customer).

3. As a plain-paper report with a title across the top of the first page, addressed to someone within the company or to someone outside.

An investigation report will probably be the biggest report you will write. It will also be the most complex, because its writing pyramid calls for two sets of writing compartments. The basic set of writing compartments is similar to the pyramid used for an incident report (see Figure 3–1). A second set of subcompartments expands the Investigation compartment. Both sets are shown in Figure 4–1 and are described here.

1. The **Summary Statement** is always necessary and has a very clear purpose: to tell the reader as quickly as possible what the problem is and how it can be overcome.

Jan Vandersteen has been examining a problem for her company. Here is her Summary Statement:

The basement flooding we experience each spring is caused by squirrels depositing rubbish in the drainpipes the previous fall. It can be corrected by placing wire mesh screens over gutter drain holes, at an installation cost of $370 and a recurring annual maintenance cost of $100.

2. The **Background** mentions facts or events that led up to the investigation, how it came to be assigned to you, and any other information you think would be useful to the reader. Jan used a heading and wrote:

Background

Since we moved into the Winston building five years ago, the basement has been flooded for about one week every spring and sometimes after particularly heavy rainfalls in the summer. Although it is a nuisance, damage has never been enough to warrant expensive investigation and repairs. But when, on July 18, management decided to use the basement for additional storage space, I was assigned by Ken Reiter to investigate the cause of the flooding and recommend a remedy. The project is urgent because the first materials to be stored in the basement – for Project 9903 – will arrive on August 10.

Figure 4-1   Writing pyramid for an investigation report

Reporting an Investigation

Summary	A very short definition of the problem and the best way to overcome it
Background	Description of the problem and the circumstances leading up to it
Investigation	How you tackled the problem, and how you think it can be resolved
Outcome/Action	The results plus what you think should be done; very brief
Evidence	Data to support the Investigation Details

Approach	What you did
Findings	What you found out
Ideas	How the problem can be overcome or resolved
Evaluation Criteria	Your evaluation criteria
Evaluation	How effective each method will be

3. The **Investigation** describes how you assessed the problem, what you discovered, what can be done to correct the problem, and which method you believe is most suitable. As shown in Figure 4–1, to organize the Investigation compartment you subdivide it into five smaller writing compartments; however, you don't have to use the subcompartment labels as headings:

a) In the **Approach,** describe what you planned to do and what you actually did:

Investigation of Water Ingress

The flooding could be caused either by an underground watercourse passing near the building, by leakage in the pipes leading down from the gutters, or by blocked weeping tiles in the building's foundation. Consequently, I visited City Hall to look at plot plans, then used a firehose to pour water onto the roof to replicate heavy rainstorm conditions.

b) In the **Findings,** describe what you discovered (the cause of the problem); in Jan Vandersteen's case, she wrote:

Inspection of city maps showed that no watercourse passes within 100 metres of the building. However, after I poured water onto the roof for three hours, a small flow of water entered the basement at the foot of a panelled wall on the east side. I removed sections of the wall and discovered a 1.5-metre-wide storage area behind it, with water flowing over the sides of a funnel fed by three drainpipes. The funnel was full of nuts, leaves, and similar debris, plus two dead squirrels. Apparently, squirrels enter the drainpipes from the gutters and use the funnel to store food for the winter.

c) In the **Ideas** compartment, describe possible methods you believe will correct the problem:

Possible Remedies

There are three ways we can stop squirrels from blocking the drainpipes:

1. Bolt wire mesh screens over each drain hole in the roof gutters, at a total cost of about $370. (See illustration in Attachment 1.)

2. Cut the drainpipes before they enter the building and connect them to new drainpipes outside the building that would feed directly onto the surrounding ground. The cost is estimated at $280.

3.   Redesign the catch basin in the basement so the three drainpipes feed directly into the main sewer without passing through the funnel. The cost is estimated at $1700. (See design in Attachment 2.)

d)   In the **Evaluation Criteria,** establish the factors you will use to evaluate the suitability of each Idea (i.e. each method, plan, or product). For example, if you are evaluating products such as automobiles or personal computers, never compare one model or product against another. First, establish your measurement criteria, which are the factors that will most influence your choice (such as the desired price, speed, efficiency, and reliability), and then *compare each model or product against the measurement criteria.* You will sound much more convincing if you compare a model or product with "desired standards" rather than against each other.

The same applies to evaluation methods for resolving a problem. First, establish your measurement criteria to identify what the best method will do or will achieve, and then assess how each method measures up to the criteria. For the water seepage problem, Jan wrote:

The remedy we select must

- be 100% effective,

- not introduce any other problems,

- cost no more than the $500 management has budgeted to rectify the problem, and

- be installed within seven working days (by August 10), when the first materials to be stored in the basement are scheduled to arrive.

It's not enough just to list your criteria: you must also justify them; otherwise your readers may question their validity. In Jan's case, she demonstrates why the maximum cost is limited to $500 and why the remedy must be implemented quickly. That the remedy must be 100% effective and not introduce other problems, however, are a given that Jan does not need to prove.

e)   In the **Evaluation,** you compare each Idea (i.e. each method for resolving the problem) against the criteria:

- **Remedy 1**   Installing wire mesh screens over the gutters can be completed within budget and the desired time frame and will be 100% effective. However, it will create an additional problem, because debris and leaves will collect on top of the wire mesh and cause rainwater to spill over the gutters onto the sidewalk beside the building. This will entail an additional annual cost of approximately $100 to clear the debris twice a year.

- **Remedy 2** Cutting the drainpipes and redirecting the rainwater away from the building can also be completed within budget and the desired time frame and will be 100% effective. However, because a city sidewalk runs along the north side of the building, this remedy will contravene city bylaw 1668, which prohibits directing rainwater onto a public walkway.

- **Remedy 3** Redesigning the catch basin will be 100% effective and will create no other problems, but it cannot be completed within the desired time frame and will exceed the budget by $1200.

4. The **Outcome/Action** compartment has two subcompartments: **Conclusions** and **Recommendations.** They should be treated as two separate paragraphs.

In the **Conclusions** subcompartment you draw conclusions based on what you have written earlier. You should never advocate what action should be taken here (that belongs in the Recommendations):

Conclusions

None of the three proposed remedies meets all of our requirements:

- Remedies 1 and 2 will cost less than $500, but both will create other problems. The wire mesh screens will collect debris and spill rainwater over the edge of the gutters. Cutting the drainpipes will contravene city bylaw 1668 by directing water onto a public sidewalk.

- Remedy 3 meets two of the criteria (it will be 100% effective and will not create further problems), but it will cost $1200 more than the budgeted funds and cannot be completed in time.

In the **Recommendations** subcompartment you state, unequivocally, what action you believe must be taken. Write your recommendations in the active voice (i.e. begin firmly with "I recommend..." or "We recommend..." rather than the wishy-washy "It is recommended..."). Jan wrote,

Recommendation

Because of its simplicity and low price, I recommend placing wire mesh screens over the drain holes at a cost of $370. I also recommend engaging Monroe Building Services to clean leaves and debris from the gutters twice a year, at a cost of $50 per cleaning.

Jan Vandersteen

It's important that the Conclusions and Recommendations *contain no surprises*. You must never introduce information that has not already been discussed earlier in the report.

Use the **Evidence** compartment to attach drawings, photographs, lists of equipment, calculations, results of tests, and detailed cost estimates, so that they do not clutter the narrative of your report and interrupt the flow of information. You can label them as *Attachments* (in which case number them "1," "2," "3," etc.) or as *Appendices* (in which case letter them "A," "B," "C," etc.). Always check that you refer to each piece of evidence within the report, as Jan Vandersteen has done in the Ideas section of her report.

Very short investigation reports do not require every writing compartment, as shown in Figure 4–2.

Figure 4-2   A short investigation report using only some writing compartments

The Furniture House

To: Derek Pritchard   From: Charles Murray
Date: April 10, 2000
Subject: Rug Damage   Complaint: Ms. V. Carson, Dover Rd.

Summary Statement

I have investigated Ms. Carson's complaint and agree she has a case. Damage has been done to her carpet, but it was partly her own fault.

Background

I called on Ms. Carson at suite 1407 - 2022 Dover Road yesterday afternoon. She showed me brown paint marks on her white carpet, which she claims were made by our service technician when he did a touch-up job on her buffet on Tuesday April 7.

Findings

The rug has about a dozen brown marks each about the size of a 25-cent piece clustered in an area 1 metre in diameter. The colour is the same as the buffet.

This morning I talked to Andy Bowen, the service technician who did the repair work. He told me that he twice warned Ms. Carson to keep her cats away from his tools and paints, but she kept insisting they were well trained and would not be a nuisance. But while he was working and she was out of the room, one of the cats put a damp paw into the brown paint powder. Andy wiped its paws, but not before it had made several marks on the rug. He told Ms. Carson what had happened, but he says she did not seem to be concerned about it.

From my examination, I agree the marks could have been made by a cat's paw.

Ideas and Outcome/ Action

It may be difficult to remove the spots because we cannot use paint remover and normal rug cleaning processes may be only partly effective. If cleaning will remove the spots, I think we should bear the cost. However, if Ms. Carson pressures us for a new rug – which she may try to do – then I suggest we hold out for a small partial cash settlement.

Charles

Figure 4-3 Writing pyramid for an evaluation report

Reporting an Evaluation

Summary	A brief synopsis of the purpose of the project, the main findings, and the outcome
Background	An introduction to the situation and the purpose and scope of the project
Project Details	A detailed description of the project, the findings, and what needs to be done
Outcome/Action	A terminal summary: it sums up the main findings and what action should be taken
Evidence	Data that supports statements in the report: charts, cost analyses, statistics, drawings

Approach	How the project was tackled
Parameters	Guidelines that were established
Findings	What was found out: the results
Evaluation	What the results mean
Suggestions	What can or needs to be done

Reporting an Evaluation

In an evaluation, you either (1) examine an existing system, method, process, or procedure to assess its value and efficiency, or (2) examine alternative plans, methods, or products to determine which is most suitable for a particular requirement. Often, the first evaluation may lead to the second. For example, a consultant examining a cost accounting procedure may show it to be inefficient, which will lead to the consultant being asked to evaluate alternative methods to identify which would be the most effective procedure to adopt.

Wendy Riverton has adapted the writing pyramid for an investigation report (see Figure 4–1) to suit an evaluation she has been conducting. Her revised writing pyramid is shown in Figure 4–3 and her six-page report *Evaluation of Telecommuting as an Employment Strategy* is shown in Figure 4–4. In her report, she evaluates an experiment that Multiple Industries Incorporated has conducted to assess the feasibility of a relatively new employment method. The project has not produced the results she anticipated, so she ends her report with a recommendation that the project be extended for another 12 months. The numbers beside the report correspond to the comments below, which in turn refer to the writing pyramid in Figure 4–3.

1. The **Summary** provides a very brief description of the whole report, primarily identifying
   - why the project was undertaken (Wendy writes: "to assess the feasibility of introducing telecommuting as an integral method of employment"),
   - the main findings ("proved inconclusive," and "can be used successfully"), and
   - what should be done next ("the project should be extended").

2. The **Background** is identified by the heading **Introduction**. It describes the factors leading up to the project and how it was initiated, and outlines the scope of the report. Wendy's introduction continues for three paragraphs.

3. Wendy provides a detailed description of the project's history because she recognizes her report will also be read by Multiple Industries' branch managers, and that some may not know about the project.

4. The "scope" of the report identifies how deeply the topic will be covered. Wendy identifies the scope of her report with the words "...telecommuting, which is defined, described, and evaluated in this report."

5. The **Project Details** start here. In her **Approach**, Wendy defines the project's three objectives and identifies how the project was handled in its early stages.

6. The **Parameters** establish the guidelines that were set for running the project and measuring its success. Wendy defines the employee job classifications to be consid-

ered for the project, how the employees' productivity will be measured, and how the success of the project is to be evaluated.

(7) Wendy's parameters continue with descriptions of the employees chosen to take part in the project. She starts by describing how they were selected and then provides a brief sketch of each person.

(8) For most reports it would be sufficient to mention only the name and job classification of each participant. Wendy includes some personal information because in later paragraphs she will draw on these details when describing whether the project was a success.

(9) A report writer normally must be completely objective when describing **Findings**. However, we recommend opening the Findings section with a brief, moderately subjective introductory remark, which in effect becomes a section Summary Statement (see Wendy's opening sentence). All of the following paragraphs must then substantiate the opening remark without allowing the report writer's personal observations to intrude. Starting each section of a long report with a Summary Statement extends the Pyramid Method to each individual part of the report.

(10) Although some of Wendy's comments in the Findings may *appear* to be subjective, in effect they are not because she is simply reporting what the employees told her about their experiences.

(11) In the **Evaluation**, a report analyzes and interprets the Findings, comments on their effect, and sometimes predicts their impact. The length of the Evaluation can vary, depending on the type of project and how clear-cut the Findings are. Wendy's Evaluation is short because the Findings were comprehensive and self-explanatory.

(12) The **Suggestions** compartment is optional. For some evaluation reports, the topic may require the report writer only to present and evaluate the results, in which case Suggestions and Recommendations are omitted. But when a report writer believes certain steps need to be taken, these steps are presented as Suggestions and summarized as Recommendations at the end of the report (see comment 15). By providing well-developed Suggestions, Wendy prepares her readers to accept her Recommendations.

(13) A report writer has considerable flexibility when arranging the Evaluation and Suggestions. The Suggestions may follow immediately after the Findings, and then the Evaluation comments on both the Findings and Suggestions. Alternatively, the Evaluation may follow immediately after the Findings (as Wendy has positioned them in her report), and then are followed by the Suggestions and a brief analysis of their value.

Figure 4-4   An evaluation report

Multiple Industries Incorporated

Evaluation of Telecommuting as an Employment Strategy

A Preliminary Report Covering the Period
November 1, 1999 to July 31, 2000

Report prepared by
Wendy K. Riverton
Manager, Human Resources

Summary

① Our pilot project to assess the feasibility of introducing telecommuting as an integral method of employment has proved inconclusive. After nine months, less than half the optimum number of participants had been recruited, which provided too small a sample on which to base a sound evaluation. Because there is sufficient evidence to show that telecommuting can be used successfully at Multiple Industries, I suggest the pilot project be extended for a further year and the range of job descriptions available for telecommuting be widened to include a broader range of employees.

Introduction

② The suggestion to incorporate telecommuting into our employment plans was proposed initially by Joe Van Nuys and Marion Hartland in 1997. It was part of a two-part proposal to test and evaluate more flexible, employee-oriented employment methods at Multiple Industries for 12 months, after which management ③ would decide whether the methods should be adopted permanently. The proposed methods were job-sharing and telecommuting. Job-sharing was tested between November 2, 1998 and October 29, 1999 and described in my report *Evaluation of Job Sharing as an Employment Option*.[1] Telecommuting is defined, described, and evaluated in this report.

④ Although we first considered the two employment methods to be complementary and planned to test them in parallel, we later decided to test them separately with different sets of participants. Job-sharing had been tried previously and reported on by other industries and the Ontario government.[2] Our report provided further evidence that job-sharing is a valid employment method, and on February 1, 2000 it was adopted as a permanent employment option.

Telecommuting (which we originally referred to as "working at home") is a newer concept and its effects have been both positively and negatively reported on elsewhere.[3] I cannot report definitive results because our experiment used too small a sample. This report, therefore, is only a preliminary assessment.

1

Figure 4-4 Continued

⑤ **Project Definition**

At the start of the project we defined telecommuting as an employment method in which selected employees work from their homes for at least 50% of the time and come into the office for less than 50% of the time. Our study had three objectives:

1. To provide an employment method that would meet the needs of employees who have difficulty adapting to regular office hours.

2. To improve personal productivity by reducing employees' travel time between their homes and the workplace.

3. To reduce the demand for office space, since an employee working at home requires a much less formal and complete office work location.

Employees participating in the telecommuting project were to receive their full salary and benefits. A computer, printer, high-speed modem, and dedicated telephone line would be installed in each home. The software would vary, depending on the individual's job requirements.

The telecommuting plan was announced to all employees in a September 15, 1999 company bulletin. To facilitate monitoring, only employees at the Willowdale plant were invited to participate in the pilot project.

⑥ **Project Parameters**

We recognized from the start that only certain job classifications were suitable for telecommuting. Primarily, these were positions that neither require a lot of equipment nor require the employee to interface frequently with other departments or employees (although with new communication technologies, we have since realized the latter is only a minor constraint). From the company's list of job classifications I identified a short list of jobs that would be eligible, mostly positions such as Software Designer, Draftsperson, and Technical Writer.

Before the project started I defined the types of employees who would be most suitable for, or who would most likely want to take part in, telecommuting. Generally, I assumed these would be single parents with young children or employees with physical limitations that affected their mobility. However, I decided not to establish any criteria that would prevent an individual from applying, other than the feasibility of transferring the person's work to a remote location.

I established that we would need a minimum of six employees to participate in the pilot project. Fewer than six would provide too small a sample with which to evaluate the efficacy of telecommuting and its suitability for company-wide use.

The most difficult parameters to establish were how we would measure employee productivity. Simply counting computer key-strokes, for example – as was done in some organizations in early tests – would seem too much like "policing." I also recognized that people who work at home in most cases would not confine

2

Figure 4-4 Continued

their working hours to a standard 8:00 a.m. to 4:30 p.m. schedule. Consequently, I decided to ask each participant to record their daily work times in a personal log book.

I recognized that the project could only be evaluated subjectively, and that it would have to be done by the employees taking part in the project and by each employee's supervisor. To implement the evaluation, I asked each participant and supervisor to submit a written report and answers to a list of questions at three-month intervals.

(7) **Project Participants**

No employees responded to the company's invitation in Bulletin 117, circulated on September 15, 1999. A second, more clearly explained bulletin was circulated on October 5 and this time I received five applications, two of which I accepted. The rejected applications were from two employees working on the assembly line and a buyer in the Purchasing Department, who held jobs I had previously defined as unsuitable for telecommuting. A third application was received three months later, after the employee had observed another employee working successfully at home. The three employees, their job positions, and their reasons for participating in the pilot project follow.

1. **Martin Pauls, CAD/CAM Designer**

(8)   Martin has been employed by Multiple Industries for seven years and is a single parent with two children who, at the start of the project, were aged 4 and 2. He had been taking the children to a daycare centre during the day, but when a child was sick he either had to take time off work or try to find a babysitter on short notice. Martin had considered job-sharing but had rejected it because he could not live on only half his salary. He started telecommuting on December 1, 1999.

2. **Natalie Taverner, Software Designer**

Natalie works in the Research and Development Department and has been with Multiple Industries for two years. She is married and has a 2-year-old daughter whom she takes to a babysitter's home while Natalie and her husband are at work. Natalie felt her daughter needed more parental attention and would have become involved in the job-sharing project if software design could have been shared. She started telecommuting on December 15, 1999.

3. **Peter Cartier, Software Designer**

Peter is paraplegic, having lost both legs in an automobile accident. He has been employed by Multiple Industries for four years. He lives alone in an apartment and takes the Speeditransit wheelchair bus, and occasionally a taxi, to work. He felt that he could be more productive and his transportation would be less costly if he could work at home. He started telecommuting on April 3, 2000, five months after the original project start date.

3

Figure 4-4 Continued

⑨ **Project Results**

The telecommuting project was only partly successful, proper evaluation having been inhibited by the low number of participants. The project started late, had only three participants after five months, and had one of the original participants withdraw from the program after the sixth month. Some brief comments on individual progress for the nine-month period November 1, 1999 to July 31, 2000 follow.

1. Martin Pauls, CAD/CAM Designer

Martin's adaptation to telecommuting is the only part of the experiment I can describe as totally successful. Martin now works at home four days a week and comes to the office for part of the fifth day. A dedicated workspace is no longer kept available for him in the Drafting Department. Both he and his supervisor report that the plan is working well and that Martin wants to continue working at home at the end of the pilot project.

⑩ Martin reports that his work hours are irregular. When his children are at home his time is limited, so he tends to work mostly in the evening. He has continued to take the children to a daycare centre. He claims his productivity has increased and his supervisor corroborates this. He has also lost no work time since starting the project.

2. Natalie Taverner, Software Designer

Natalie's adaptation to telecommuting has been less successful. She reverted to regular employment after only five months. She stated that she could not obtain the in-depth involvement necessary for complex software development when she was constantly being interrupted by her child, and that working in the evenings proved impractical because then both her husband and her daughter were at home. Consequently, she became frustrated because she could not achieve what she wanted to do, and she became increasingly exasperated with herself and her family. As a result, she began to spend more time working in the office and much less time working at home.

3. Peter Cartier, Software Designer

Unfortunately, Peter's experiment with telecommuting has not worked as well as he had anticipated, but for an unpredictable reason. At first Peter reported he was very pleased with the work arrangements, particularly because he had only minor problems communicating with the office "at a distance" and had said that software design is an ideal occupation for anyone working in the privacy and silence of an apartment. His manager reported that for the first two months Peter's productivity was exemplary, but over the past six weeks the quality and quantity of his work has declined.

In his July 31 report Peter noted that as time progressed it became increasingly difficult to "...wind myself up each day to start working at the terminal. I

4

Figure 4-4   Continued

kept (mentally) kicking myself because this was something I'd wanted to do, and now it didn't seem to be working for me." He then realized he was missing the interaction between himself and fellow employees. By working at home he had virtually cut himself off from contact with people during the day and had become almost a "shut-in." He is still working on the project but doubts whether he will continue working at home for more than another month.

⑪ As a result, after only nine months our pilot telecommuting project has been narrowed to only one successful participant. This means we must either discontinue the project or extend it for another year and broaden it to include a wider range of participants. The latter would be preferable, since our success with one participant has shown that with the right people and the right circumstances the concept is feasible.

Broadening the Scope of the Project

⑫ I have re-examined our list of job classifications and have identified several job titles which I previously considered to be inappropriate for telecommuting, but which on second thought might be suitable:

- **Assembly Technician** Production manager Frank Hobbs and I have discussed the possibility of allowing some assembly work to be done away from the plant, rather like a "cottage industry." Although much production and assembly work must be done in the plant because it requires special equipment or a dust-free environment, there are some tasks, such as small cabinet pre-assembly, which could be done in an employee's home.

- **Purchasing Agent (Buyer)** Buyers spend much of their time on the telephone, making enquiries, requesting price quotations, and placing orders. Almost all internal purchase requisitions reach the buyers electronically. They then create a purchase order and submit it to the supplier either electronically or by fax. Thus, buyers could readily work from home except when they need to interview a supplier personally. Interviews could be arranged for a particular day of the week and held in-plant. I have discussed the practicality of a Buyer telecommuting four days a week with Chief Purchasing Agent Alan Cairns, and he agrees that it could work.

- **Service Technician** Service Manager Dana Hill endorses the idea. She suggests it would be faster for a technician to go to a client's office directly from home rather than have to come first to the office to pick up orders. Service orders would be sent to the technician's home computer.

- **Technical Writer** Technical writers are ideal telecommuting candidates because their work demands long, solitary hours at a computer terminal.

- **Sales Representative** Paul Davis says that many Sales Representatives already go to clients directly from their homes. To include them in the telecommuting project would formalize what is already an informal working arrangement.

Figure 4-4 Continued

⑬ Undoubtedly there are other jobs which might suit a work-at-home arrangement, and each will have to be evaluated individually. I believe we will have to be much less arbitrary than when we first decided which jobs would be suitable for telecommuting.

Although we could realize an additional source of telecommuting participants by extending the study to include employees at all of Multiple Industries' branches, for the pilot project I still believe participants should come from head office. I need to have direct contact with them and must be available to monitor their individual progress. We need to identify these additional project participants by September 29, so arrangements for them to start telecommuting will be complete by November 1, 2000 – the start date for the second year of the pilot project.

Conclusions

⑭ Too few employees took part in the pilot telecommuting project to provide a sufficiently large sample for evaluation. A preliminary analysis shows the concept can work, with the right employee, under the right circumstances.

Our original definition of Multiple Industries' job classifications that are suitable for telecommuting is too narrow and too rigid. It needs to be broadened to include a wider range of positions.

Recommendations

⑮ I recommend extending the telecommuting project for 12 months, starting November 1, 2000 and ending October 31, 2001, and continuing to select participants only from the Willowdale plant. I also recommend making a concerted effort between September 1 and October 31 to attract a minimum of six employees to take part in the project, and drawing those employees from a much wider range of job classifications.

References ⑯

1. Wendy K. Riverton, *Evaluation of Job-Sharing as an Employment Option*, Multiple Industries Incorporated, Toronto, Ontario, December 5, 1999.

2. *Job-Sharing As a Means of Reducing Unemployment*, Department of Labor, Government of Ontario, Report No. 9416, June 19, 1996.

3. Francesca Willomen, "Working at Home Has Benefits and Pitfalls," *Atlantic Canada Business*, 24:7, July 1997.

Wendy Riverton

Wendy Riverton
Manager, Human Resources
August 15, 2000

6

⑭ The **Outcome/Action** compartment starts here, and is divided into two subcompartments, each with its own heading: **Conclusions** and **Recommendations**. (You may know this part of an Investigation or Evaluation Report as the *Terminal Summary*.) The Conclusions are short and simply summarize the main features of the Findings, Evaluation, and Suggestions. Wendy's Conclusions are successful because she presents only the main outcomes. She writes that

- "too few employees took part,"

- "the concept can work,"

- the "original definition of ... job classifications ... [was] too narrow,"

- the "definition ... needs to be broadened."

The Conclusions must never introduce any information that has not been discussed in earlier parts of the report.

⑮ The **Recommendations**, which also are optional, must state clearly what action the report writer believes must be taken. Wendy starts her Recommendations correctly by using the confident and assertive active voice and the introductory phrase "I recommend...." She does not write in the passive voice: "It is recommended that...."

⑯ The **References** list documents that Wendy drew on when making specific statements in her report.

Reporting a Comparative Analysis

You may have to write a report in which you must evaluate several plans, methods, sites, or products and then make a recommendation. But before you can do that you need to compare the alternatives and discuss which is most suitable to adopt. Sometimes such an evaluation is called a justification; more often it is called a comparative analysis.

You can write a comparative analysis as a primarily *objective* presentation of alternatives, in which case your preference for a particular plan or product does not become apparent until the very end of the report, when you make your recommendation. Or you can write it as a primarily *subjective* presentation of alternatives, in which case your preference for a particular plan or product is evident much earlier in the report. These two approaches are illustrated in Figure 4–5.

An effective comparative analysis has three main parts, in which you

- identify and describe the items to be compared (the alternatives),

- establish the factors that will influence the final selection (the selection criteria), and

- evaluate each of the alternatives.

Figure 4–5 shows how the sequence in which you present these parts depends on whether you are writing an objective or subjective comparative analysis.

Figure 4-5   Alternative writing pyramids for a comparative analysis

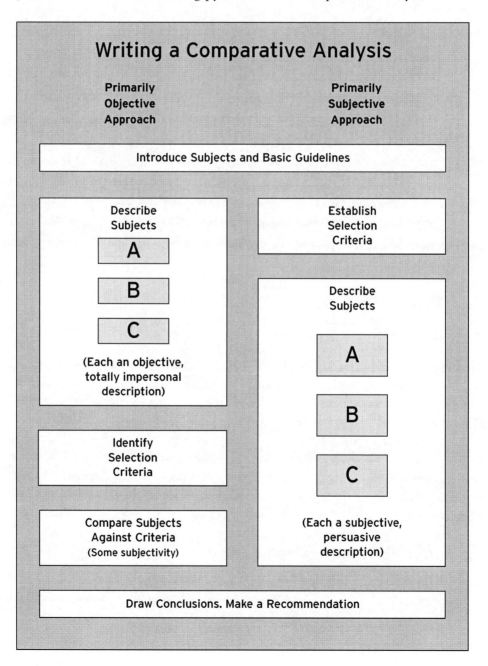

An Objective Comparative Analysis

Start with a Summary Statement (not shown in the figure) in which you identify the need for the analysis and state what approach or method should be adopted or which product should be purchased. For example,

> I have evaluated four sport utility vehicle models to determine which we should purchase to replace our existing three survey crew vehicles. The best choice is the four-door Nabuchi Tarragon with all-wheel drive, at a lease price of $427 a month over four years. The buyout price at the end of the lease will be $8500.

Introduce the Comparative Analysis

Identify the methods or products you evaluated and state why they were chosen. We recommend you limit your list to no more than four alternatives. If, during your investigation, you examined more than four, divide them into two groups:

1. Those that had constraints and were eliminated early in your study. Describe them briefly and explain why you eliminated them.

2. Those that had clear possibilities and were examined in detail. Describe them briefly and explain why you included them in your evaluation.

Describe the Alternatives

Work your way down the left-hand column of Figure 4–5, describing the features, capabilities, and cost of each alternative *without making any personal comments or offering an opinion about its suitability*. Your intent is simply to *tell* about each alternative:

> The four-door Tarragon is built at the Nabuchi plant in Richmond, Virginia. It has a wheelbase of 2.26 m (89 in.), a cargo area of 1.23m³ (38.56 cu ft) with all four seats in position and 2.38 m³ (74.38 cu ft) with the rear seats folded forward. Entry to the cargo area is through a full-size rear door that is hinged on the right and opens sideways. The floor of the cargo area is 0.72 m (27 in.) from the ground and has no lip, so that large objects can be slid directly in and out of the compartment.

Suppose you had written the final two sentences like this:

> Entry to the cargo area is easy, because the full-size rear door is hinged on the right, and so opens sideways. The floor is a comfortable 0.72 m (27 in.) from the ground. Because it has no lip, it permits you to slide large objects in and out without having to lift them over an awkward coaming. This will be particularly useful when loading our survey equipment.

Now you've introduced opinions:

- "Entry is...*easy*,"
- "a *comfortable* 0.72 cm (27 in.),"
- "an *awkward* coaming,"
- "This *will be particularly useful....*"

In so doing, you have commented on the product and you are no longer just *telling* about it. Your credibility as an objective writer would be weakened because of the interjected opinions.

The sequence in which you list the alternatives is also important. You may list them in order from the best choice to the least likely choice. Or you may list them in reverse order, starting with the least likely choice and ending with the best choice. However, we do not recommend that you inform your readers of the sequence: it's better to allow them to sense it intuitively.

Establish Your Selection Criteria

Before you evaluate each alternative, you need to identify what factors will influence your selection. These factors might include cost, accessibility, availability, convenience, and ease and speed of operation. For example,

The three sport utility vehicles we lease must

- **be acquired within a total lease price of $1200 a month to conform with the budget authorized at the October 1999 board meeting;**
- **have a minimum of 2.21 m³ (69 cu ft) of cargo space to accommodate the equipment, materials, and personal effects of a two-person survey crew;**
- **have a minimum of 228 mm (9 in.) of road clearance to permit access to rough off-road terrain; and**
- **have a large-enough gasoline tank to travel 560 km (350 miles) between fillings, for off-road surveys.**

Each criterion you establish should be more than a simple statement like: "They must be acquired within a total lease price of $1200 a month." You also need to show *why* each criterion is important; otherwise your readers may question why you have established it. In other words, always *prove* your criteria: "They must be acquired within a total lease price of $1200 a month to conform with the budget authorized at the October 1999 board meeting."

Evaluate the Alternatives

It's in writing the evaluation that many writers make a mistake: they try to compare the alternatives against each other. This creates two problems:

- They get tangled up in their writing, often producing a confusing analysis.

- Their bias, whether intended or otherwise, tends to show.

A far simpler and more convincing way to evaluate each alternative is to *compare it against the criteria* established in the previous step. Again, remember that in an objective comparative analysis you must *not* introduce any comments or opinions. For example, it's acceptable to write

> **The Nabuchi Tarragon meets three of the four criteria: it has sufficient cargo space for carrying two surveyors and their equipment; it has sufficient road clearance for off-road travel; and it has a gasoline tank large enough to travel 560 km (350 miles). However, it exceeds the lease budget by $27 per vehicle a month.**

It's unacceptable to insert qualifying comments and write:

> **The Nabuchi Tarragon meets more criteria than any of the other vehicles we evaluated: it has more than enough cargo space for two surveyors and their equipment; it has 38 mm (1.5 in.) more road clearance than the best of the other vehicles; and its excellent combination of gasoline economy and an unusually large gasoline tank permits far more than the minimum 560 km (350 miles) travel required by our off-road survey crews. Although it exceeds the lease budget by $27 per vehicle a month, the excellent performance record of this unique vehicle warrants finding additional funds to acquire it.**

Here, the opinions have created a subjective rather than an objective description.

Draw Conclusions

At this point you summarize the key outcomes of the evaluation. Now you can insert your comments and opinions and compare the pros and cons of the alternatives:

> **Of the four sport utility vehicle models I evaluated, only the Carivan can be leased within the confines of the $1200 per month lease budget. This vehicle, however, has only 221 mm (8.7 in.) road clearance and has the smallest cargo capacity of all four vehicles. On those grounds, I considered it the least practical vehicle to lease.**
>
> **On first examination, the Roadmaster PUV seemed to meet all our requirements. It has...**

Subjective statements like this are acceptable because they are based on the objective evaluations discussed in previous paragraphs. However, they must never introduce anything that has not been discussed earlier in the report: the conclusions must *present no surprises*. And they must never state what action should be taken: that belongs only in the recommendations.

Make a Recommendation

Using the outcome evident in your conclusions, tell your readers what action needs to be taken. Use a positive, definite, firm tone:

> **I recommend that we lease three Nabuchi Tarragon sport utility vehicles with four doors and all-wheel drive at $427 a month per vehicle, with a four-year term and a buyout price at the end of the lease of $8500.**

For another example of the objective approach, see Jan Vandersteen's report investigating the cause of and remedy for water ingress in Multiple Industries' basement in the "Reporting an Investigation" section of this chapter.

A Subjective Comparative Analysis

In a subjective comparative analysis

- the Summary Statement and the Introduction remain the same as those for an objective analysis,
- the Selection Criteria compartment is moved forward, before describing the alternatives,
- the Compare Subjects compartment is eliminated, and
- the Conclusions and Recommendation compartments remain the same.

See the right-hand side of Figure 4–5.

Establish Your Selection Criteria

This is the first major difference between the objective and subjective methods: you define your selection criteria *before* you describe the alternatives, listing them just as you would for an objective analysis.

Describe the Alternatives

The second difference is that you can voice your opinions much earlier in the report, which makes it subjective. The description of each alternative becomes more detailed because you compare its attributes against the criteria and may comment on its positive and negative aspects. Here is an example:

> **The four-door Nabuchi Tarragon is built at the company's Richmond, Virginia plant and meets or exceeds 90% of our requirements. It has a wheelbase of 2.26 m (89 in.) and a cargo space of 1.23 m³ (38.6 cu ft) with all four seats in position and 2.38 m³ (74.38 cu ft) with the rear seats folded forward; this is 0.17 m³ (5.40 cu ft) more than the minimum required. Although this limits occupancy to only a driver and one passenger, it will not pose a problem except in heavily wooded areas when we need additional crew members to clear brush (about 5% of our survey activity). For**

these occasions we normally hire crew members locally, and in future we can stipulate that one brush clearer has his or her own transportation.

Entry to the cargo area is through a full-size rear door that is hinged on the right and opens sideways, providing easy access for even the largest pieces of survey equipment. The floor of the cargo area is 0.72 m (27 in.) above the ground and has no lip, so that large equipment can be slid directly in and out of the compartment.

You still do not compare the alternatives against each other; however, you can still arrange them from best choice to least likely choice, or least likely choice to best choice. But don't tell your readers you have arranged them in a particular sequence.

Because the description of each alternative *also evaluates it*, you can omit the Compare Subjects Against Criteria compartment of the objective approach and go straight into the Conclusions and Recommendations.

Draw Conclusions and Make Recommendations

Your Conclusions and Recommendations are written in exactly the same way as in an objective analysis. Remember, never surprise your reader by introducing new information in either the Conclusions or the Recommendations.

Which Type of Analysis Should You Use?

Whether you choose to write a primarily objective or subjective analysis depends on which approach you are most comfortable writing and which most suits the reader. Most beginning report writers find the objective approach easier to write. More experienced report writers, who feel comfortable using the first person and offering their opinions throughout the narrative, often find they can write a subjective analysis with confidence.

The key really lies in how well you know your readers and how readily you can anticipate their expectations. If you know your readers well enough to know they will be "in tune" with your conclusions and recommendations, then you should be able to use the subjective approach with confidence. If, however, you are unsure of your readers' possible reactions, or are aware that your readers have fixed opinions that are contrary to your recommendations, then you would do better to use the objective approach. Writing an objective analysis lets your readers see you as an unbiased and impartial report writer. If you use the subjective approach, the reader may be "turned off" by your seeming partiality for one alternative, and have difficulty accepting your conclusions and recommendations.

You can use these guidelines not only for writing investigation and evaluation reports, but also for writing business and technical proposals in which you offer your readers several choices and recommend one for their approval.

CHAPTER 5

Writing Proposals

There are three types of proposal, each with a different function:

- Suggestions and short informal proposals.
- Semiformal proposals.
- Formal proposals.

Informal Proposals

Informal proposals offer an idea and discuss why it should be implemented. Most informal proposals are written as memorandums between, say, an employee and a supervisor within the same department, or between two people (usually supervisors) in different departments. In each case the writer believes there is a better way to do something and proposes trying the new method. Typical informal proposals might be

- a suggestion from a staff member that the department buy a new graphics software package,
- a proposal to stagger break- or lunchtimes, to avoid lineups at the cafeteria counter, or
- a request to attend a course or conference (a request is, in effect, a proposal).

Semiformal Proposals

Semiformal proposals can range from one or two pages to 30 or more pages. They may occasionally be written as a memorandum, but more often are written as a letter. If the proposal is long enough or important enough, it may be preceded by a title page or have the heading PROPOSAL followed by a title centred at the top of the first page of text. In either case, it is sent to the reader with a cover letter.

A semiformal proposal may suggest ways to increase productivity, improve a situation, resolve a problem, or conduct research. For example,

- a request from a production manager suggesting that the company research space for a new production line,

- a recommendation by a consultant proposing that a client reduce overhead costs by amalgamating two departments,

- a proposal by a manager of field operations asking the company to supply portable computers with built-in fax modems to the construction crew supervisors, or

- a letter from a consultant specializing in the effects of high noise levels, proposing that the local airport authority measure sound levels under the approach path to the main runway, where residents complain that aircraft flying overhead disturb their sleep.

Formal Proposals

Formal proposals are large and often multiple-volume documents designed to impress upon the government or a major organization, such as Ontario Hydro, that the proposing company has the capability to carry out an important, often multi-million-dollar task or project. They are substantial because they describe in detail what will be done, how it will be done, who will be responsible for specific aspects of the work, and why the proposing company has the potential to complete the project on time, within budget, and to the client's satisfaction.

Formal proposals are normally prepared in response to a *Request for Proposal* (RFP) and are usually written as a team effort, operating under a tight delivery deadline. The RFP often defines exactly how the proposal is to be organized, what topics must be covered and in what sequence, and, sometimes, how many pages are to be devoted to each topic. Typical examples would be

- a proposal to provide training services for a company with branches nationwide,

- a proposal to research ways of improving a bank's automatic teller services for customers, and

- a proposal to refurbish mobile communication systems for National Defence.

Because formal reports are beyond the scope of this book, this chapter will concentrate on preparing and presenting informal and semiformal proposals.

Impact on Reader

The quality of a company's proposal often influences its acceptance. When Marie Havelock wanted to build a family room and a three-piece bathroom in her basement, she invited three renovation contractors to give her an estimate. They each visited her and she gave them a carefully drawn sketch of her ideas. Contractor A quoted a price over the telephone. Contractor B delivered a handwritten letter saying: *Our price for installing the family room and bathroom in your basement, as per your drawing, will be $XXX, GST and Provincial Sales Tax extra.* Contractor C mailed her a word-processed letter describing how the work would be done, how quickly the job would be completed, and what materials would be used. The proposal included a detailed sketch and some recommendations for improving the plan Marie had provided. It also stated that the contractor would clean up and remove all construction debris from the site. The prices the contractors quoted were similar.

Marie gave the job to contractor C because the detailed information in the letter, plus its appearance, convinced her Contractor C would be the most efficient. Perhaps the other two contractors might have done a better job, but the impression they created seemed to indicate otherwise.

Proposal Design

The Pyramid Method applies to proposals, just as it does to reports. The number of compartments within the pyramid depends on the complexity of the proposal. All proposals, regardless of their length, contain

1. a **Summary** that describes briefly what is being proposed and identifies any significant factors (such as cost),

2. **Background** information that outlines why the proposal was prepared,

3. definitive **Details** that describe what needs to be done, how it will be done, what the results will be, and, sometimes, why the proposer has the capability to do the job (this is the body of the proposal),

4. an **Action Statement** that requests approval to go ahead or for the reader to make a decision or perform a specific action, and

5. **Appendices** that contain detailed evidence to support statements made in the body of the proposal.

Plan for an Informal Proposal

The writing plan for an informal proposal is shown in Figure 5–1. This is the form of proposal you will most often write in-house:

The five parts of the writing plan are described in more detail in Table 5–1.

The memo-style informal proposal in Figure 5–2 was written for an in-house audience. The writing compartments can be readily identified, yet the writer did not feel that she had to adhere rigidly to them. This "comfortableness" makes the proposal easy to read.

Plan for a Basic Semiformal Proposal

The writing plan for a semiformal proposal is similar to that for an informal proposal, but the **Details** compartment is expanded to have two more subcompartments, as shown in Figure 5–3. There also is an additional compartment, known as the **Attachments** or **Appendices**, which holds data that supports statements made in the body of the proposal. Generally, Attachments are used for semiformal proposals and Appendices are used for formal proposals. (Attachments are normally numbered 1, 2, 3, etc. and

Figure 5-1   Writing plan for a suggestion or informal proposal

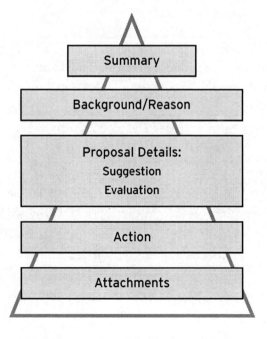

Summary	• Briefly describes the idea or plan
Background/Reason	• Describes the circumstances and why the proposed idea or plan is necessary
Proposal Details: **Suggestion** **Evaluation**	• Describes what the idea or plan will achieve, how it will be implemented, and how effective it will be
Action	• Makes a request for approval
Attachments	• Provides evidence to support your proposal

Compartment	Contents
Table 5-1	The parts of an informal proposal
Summary	What you want to do or want done (this is your main message).
Background	The circumstances that led up to your writing the proposal — all the history.
Details	A detailed description of • the proposed change or improvements, why they are necessary, and what they will cost; • an evaluation of the viability of the proposed changes and the effect they will have, including any problems that will evolve and how they will be overcome.
Action	A firm statement identifying what you want done, when, and by whom.
Attachments	Supporting data such as drawings, plans, cost estimates, and computer-generated statistics.

Appendices are labelled A, B, C, etc.) Table 5–2 describes in more detail what is included in each part of the writing plan.

The four-page semiformal proposal in Figure 5–4 was written by Mavis Hamilton of Floral West Imports Ltd. When writing the proposal, Mavis adopted the pyramid writing plan illustrated in Figure 5–3 and described in Table 5–2, making some adaptations to suit her particular situation. The following numbered paragraphs comment on Mavis's proposal and correspond to the numbers beside the figure.

(1) This paragraph is Mavis's **Summary**. She identifies the key features of her proposal and indents the paragraph from both margins to draw the reader's eye to it.

(2) Not everyone likes to put the total cost right up front. Some people fear that, if the cost seems high, the reader may not read the remainder of the proposal. Mavis counters this by saying: "The cost is what readers *most* want to know! They are going to search for it anyway, so I might as well place it where they can find it."

(3) The four paragraphs of the Introduction form Mavis's **Background** compartment. She starts by establishing her terms of reference (i.e. the purpose for writing the proposal).

(4) In this and the next paragraph, she describes the restaurants to demonstrate to her reader (who knows all this) that *she* fully understands what has to be done.

Figure 5-2   An informal proposal prepared for an in-house reader

Memorandum

To:	Vince Warchuk, Manager, Production	**From:**	Tara Williamson, Supervisor, PC Lab
Date:	June 23, 2000	**Subject:**	PC Lab Audiovisual Equipment Purchase

Summary
Statement

I propose purchasing a Nabuchi 2100 television set with integrated VCR for installation in the PC Lab, and buying the *4Tell* 4.6 video training program for use by staff converting to the *4Tell* software. The cost will be $1807.85, taxes included.

Background

The software manufacturer provided hands-on training in a classroom setting from March 30 to April 3, following installation of the new software. However, over the next two years we will still need to provide training on a continuing but sporadic basis for about 24 existing staff who will convert to the new software, and for future new hires. Sending employees to Crandell Computers, who installed the software and did the previous training, will cost $145 per person, which will result in a minimum $3480 training expense (for 24 employees).

Details

I have evaluated the 95-minute training video and it is not only an excellent production but also a very effective training tool. It's entitled "Hands-on with *4Tell*" and is divided into 14 convenient learning modules, each about seven minutes long. I also had an employee who is not experienced with *4Tell* evaluate it while working simultaneously on a PC, and he also was enthusiastic.

I plan to position the integrated TV/VCR immediately beside computer station 21, the last station in row 2. To avoid the audio affecting other computer users, I have included two cushioned headphone sets in my estimate. Specific purchase details are listed on the attachment. The cost breakdown is

1.	TV/VCR: Nabuchi 2100	$1085.00
2.	Headphones: TSR model 40, qty 2	95.00
3.	Cable junction box	24.95
4.	Video program	395.00
		1599.95
	GST	111.95
	Prov Tax	95.95
		$1807.85

Action

May I have your approval to use $1807.85 from the capital equipment budget to purchase the TV/VCR and accompanying equipment?

Tara Williamson

Tara Williamson
Supervisor, PC Lab

Figure 5-3   The writing plan for a semiformal proposal

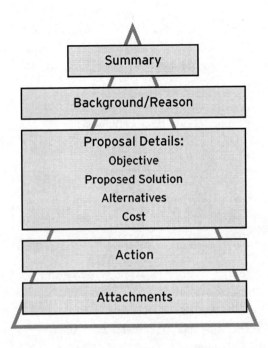

- Briefly describes what is being proposed

- Describes the circumstances and the people involved

- Gives a detailed description of what will be achieved, how it will be achieved, what alternatives are available, and why the proposal should be implemented

- Makes a strong request for approval

- Provides data to support statements made in the body of the proposal

⑤ In this single sentence Mavis describes her **Approach** and, simultaneously, the scope of the proposal. (The three compartments, *Purpose, Situation,* and *Scope,* should be present in the Introduction to all longer reports and proposals.) In her Approach she is also telling her reader that the *Proposed Solution, Alternatives,* and *Cost* will be described twice: once for each type of restaurant.

⑥Ⓐ In the remainder of page 2, Mavis describes specifically what she will do to provide the service desired for the first set of restaurants.

⑦Ⓐ In this paragraph she describes alternatives the reader may choose to adopt.

⑧Ⓐ Here she provides two costs: one for the Proposed Solution and one covering the Alternatives.

⑥Ⓑ Now Mavis describes the service she will provide for the second set of restaurants.

⑦Ⓑ Here she offers an alternative.

⑧Ⓑ Again she provides two costs: one for the Proposed Solution and one for the Alternative.

⑨ Because there are several options, Mavis summarizes them in a table to help the reader quickly grasp the breakdown of Alternatives and their Cost.

Table 5-2	The parts of a semiformal proposal
Compartment	**Contents**
Summary	A synopsis of the key points of your proposal. It should identify the purpose, main advantages, result(s), and probably the cost(s) (this information is drawn from the Background, Details, and Action compartments). In more formal proposals, the Summary may be called the **Abstract**.
Background/Reason	A description of the situation, condition, or problem that demands attention and the circumstances leading up to it. This part is often called the **Introduction**.
Proposal Details	An introductory statement followed by four subcompartments:
	1. The **Objective** defines what needs to be achieved to improve the situation or condition, or to resolve the problem, and establishes the criteria that must be met. The Objective may also be positioned at the end of the Introduction.
	2. The **Proposed Solution** offers what the writer considers to be the best way to achieve the objective. It includes a full description of the solution, the expected result or improvement, how the solution will be implemented, its advantages and disadvantages, and its cost.
	3. The **Alternatives** compartment describes alternatives to the proposed solution.
	4. The **Cost** identifies the total cost and, sometimes, secondary costs, depending on whether there are alternatives the reader may adopt. Often, only the total cost is shown here and a breakdown of costs is placed in the Attachments.
Action Statement	A recommendation of what action needs to be taken. It is often called **Recommendations** and needs to be written in strong, positive terms.
Attachments	A collection of drawings, sketches, cost analyses, spreadsheets, etc. that provide evidence to establish the validity of statements made in the body of the proposal.

Figure 5-4   A semiformal business proposal

Floral West Imports Ltd.
470 Langley Avenue
PO Box 87061 North Vancouver Postal Station
North Vancouver BC V7L 4L6

Proposal for Supplying Tropical Plants
to Pacific Restaurants Limited

Prepared for

Mr. David Wing Lee,
General Operations Manager
Pacific Restaurants Limited

① We are proposing to supply Pacific Restaurants Limited with tropical plants for its "tropical rain forest" theme restaurants, and North American plants for its "Pacific Nook" restaurants. The plants in the rain forest restaurants will be rotated every two weeks to achieve a lush, constantly changing scene. Those in the Pacific Nook restaurants will remain, but will be trimmed and watered regularly and replaced before any signs of wilting occur. The cost for providing this service will be either
② $1305 or $1365 per month, depending on the level of service.

③ **Introduction**   In a letter dated August 24, 2000, and at a subsequent meeting on September 4, Mr. David Wing Lee, General Operations Manager of Pacific Restaurants Limited, asked Floral West Imports for a proposal to supply and maintain plants in its 20 Greater Vancouver area restaurants. The contract would last for 12 months starting October 2000.

④ There are two types of restaurants. The four "tropical rain forest" theme restaurants comprise

- *The Rain Forest* on Denman Street, Vancouver,

- *The Occasional Shower* on West Broadway, Vancouver,

- *The Samoan Retreat* in New Westminster, and

- *The Barbary Coast* in Horseshoe Bay.

These restaurants are to be filled entirely with lush tropical plants.

The sixteen smaller restaurants, called *Pacific Nooks*, have various locations in Vancouver, Burnaby, and West Vancouver. They are to have a selection of North American plants.

1

Figure 5-4 Continued

⑤   Our proposal is divided into two parts: one covering the tropical theme restaurants and the other focusing on the smaller *Pacific Nooks.*

⑥Ⓐ **Plants for**   Lush foliage plants are essential if the "tropical rain forest" theme
the Tropical   is to be maintained realistically. We propose to provide 400 plants
Theme   in three height ranges: 60 from 1.20 to 2.00 m, 200 from 0.75 to
Restaurants   0.20 m, and 140 from 0.40 to 0.75 m. All will be bushy plants with leafy internal growth.

We plan to install 240 of these plants in *The Rain Forest*, because it is considerably larger than and holds 60% more customers than the other three restaurants. Fifty of these plants will be from the largest group (1.20 to 2.00 m).

Our plan to distribute the remaining plants comprises

- 60 to *The Occasional Shower,*

- 60 to *The Samoan Retreat,*

- 40 to *The Barbary Coast.*

• **Achieving a**   The original plan, discussed at the September 3 meeting, was to
Changing   replace the tropical plants every three weeks to ensure that
Scene   customers see a continually changing scene. Our analysis, however, showed this would be prohibitively expensive. Consequently we searched for an alternative method that would achieve a comparable impression.

Our plan is to rotate approximately one-third of the plants from one restaurant to another every 10 days. This will provide each restaurant with a complete change of plants every 20 days. By starting with different types of plants in each restaurant, and with a carefully planned schedule, we can avoid duplication and provide considerable variety over a 60-day period.

• **Plant**   We will water, trim, and inspect the plants every fifth day, usually
Maintenance   in the morning by arrangement with the restaurant manager. Any wilting plants will be replaced immediately.

⑦Ⓐ • **Achieving**   If the restaurant managers feel that the number of tropical plants
an Even   does not provide sufficiently dense foliage, we can increase the
Bushier   density relatively inexpensively by placing up to 20% of synthetic
Effect   leafy plants among the live plants in the "background" settings. When this is done judiciously, the difference between the live and

2

Figure 5-4 Continued

synthetic plants cannot be detected. For this option, we suggest the following distribution of synthetic plants:

- 24 for *The Rain Forest,*
- 12 each for *The Occasional Shower* and *The Samoan Retreat,*
- 8 for *The Barbary Coast.*

(8A) **• Cost**

The fee for providing this service will be $785 per month, with a minimum 12-month contract. The price includes provision of the 400 plants and any replacements required during the term of the contract, rotation of one-third of the plants every 10 days, and full maintenance of the plants every 5 days.

If we also provide synthetic plants, the price will be $15 per plant for a total one-time cost of $840.

At the end of the contract, we will remove all live plants and clean all containers. If synthetic plants are purchased, they will remain the property of Pacific Restaurants Limited.

(6B) **North American Plants for the Pacific Nooks**

The 16 Pacific Nooks each need 12 hanging plants, for a total of 192 plants. They will be primarily ferns and vines that require low light levels, and they will be supplied in 300-mm-diameter decorative bowls, each suspended by a woven macramé hanger, which we will supply.

(7B) **• Plant Maintenance**

We will inspect, trim, and water the plants every five days, and will replace any that are wilting or appear diseased. Although Pacific Restaurants' requirements do not call for regular replacement of the plants, we could rotate them between restaurants at a nominal cost, as part of our regular maintenance service.

(8B)

Our price for providing and maintaining the plants for a minimum 12-month period will be $520 per month. If plant rotation is required, the additional fee will be $60, for a total of $580 per month.

At the end of the contract, we will remove the plants and clean all containers.

(9) **Overall Cost Considerations**

The table summarizes our price quote. Pacific Restaurants will have the option to change the arrangements at any time during the term of the contract.

3

Figure 5-4 Continued

Service	Cost per month	One-time Cost
Supply, maintain, and rotate plants in 4 tropical theme restaurants	$785	
Supply and maintain plants in 16 *Pacific Nooks*	$520	
Subtotal	**$1305**	
Optional service: Install synthetic plants in theme restaurants		$840
Optional service: Rotate plants between *Pacific Nook* restaurants	$60	
Total	**$1365**	**$840**

If Pacific Restaurants chooses to extend the contract into subsequent years, the cost will be 20% less for year two, and 25% less for year three.

⑩ **To Sum Up**   Our proposal will provide a lush setting for Pacific Restaurants' tropical theme restaurants, and a fresh, pleasant appearance for the company's *Pacific Nook* restaurants. I will gladly provide more information and answer any questions concerning our proposal.

⑪ *Mavis J. Hamilton*

Mavis J. Hamilton
President

Floral West Imports Ltd.
September 7, 2000

4

⑩ As the table has already provided a terminal summary, she concludes with an **Outcome** rather than an Action Statement. In such cases, an Action Statement would be more likely to appear in the cover letter accompanying the proposal.

⑪ Mavis's proposal is a good illustration of how to use Information Design to create an effective proposal. See pages 103 to 110 for ideas about information design.

Plan for a Comprehensive Semiformal Proposal

A comprehensive semiformal proposal differs from the previous semiformal proposal in several ways:

- It usually deals with a more complex situation, such as a problem or an unsatisfactory condition, for which it proposes a solution or resolution.
- It discusses the circumstances in more detail.
- It establishes definitive criteria for the proposed changes.
- It frequently offers alternatives rather than just a single suggestion.
- It analyzes the proposed alternatives in-depth.
- It has a more formal appearance.

The writing compartments for a comprehensive semiformal proposal are shown in Figure 5–5. They contain the following information:

1. The **Summary** briefly describes the main highlights of the proposal, mostly drawn from the **Background, Proposal Details,** and **Outcome/Action** compartments. If headings are used in the proposal, this compartment is titled *Summary* or *Abstract*.

2. The **Background** compartment introduces the problem, situation, or unsatisfactory condition, and outlines the circumstances leading up to it. It is usually titled *Introduction*.

3. The **Proposal Details** start with the **Objective**, which defines what needs to be achieved to resolve the problem and establishes **Criteria** for an ideal solution. This information may be included as part of the *Introduction* or preceded by a heading of its own, such as *Requirements* or *Criteria*.

4. **The Plan** describes, in-depth, how the problem can be resolved or the situation improved. It comprises
   - a description of the solution,
   - the result or improvement it will achieve,
   - how it will be implemented,
   - its advantages and disadvantages, and
   - its cost.

Figure 5-5 Writing plan for a comprehensive semiformal proposal

Summary	A synopsis of the proposal's main features, often including the cost	
Background	The circumstances leading up to the proposal being written	
		Objective — What the proposal will achieve
		Criteria — Guidelines that were established
Proposal Details	A detailed description of what will be done	The Plan — What will be done, how it will be done, advantages, and costs
		Alternatives — What other options are available
		Evaluation — A comparison of each alternative against the established criteria
Outcome/Action	A summing-up (in long proposals, a restatement of the key features)	
Evidence	Attachments or appendices, such as charts, cost analyses, statistics, drawings	

5. If there are **Alternatives,** they are arranged in descending order of suitability. This and the previous compartment may be preceded by a single heading, such as *Methods for Increasing Productivity*, or by several descriptive headings, one for each alternative.

6. The **Evaluation** compartment analyzes and compares the alternative solutions, with particular reference to the criteria established in the **Objective.** It may briefly discuss the effects of

    - adopting the proposed solution,

    - adopting each of the alternative solutions, and

    - adopting none of the solutions (i.e. taking no action).

7. The **Outcome** should be divided into two compartments:

    - **Conclusions,** which summarize the key result(s).

    - **Recommendations,** which state clearly what action should be taken. Recommendations should be worded in strong, positive terms and should be titled *Recommendation(s)*.

8. The **Evidence** compartment, if used, contains detailed analyses, test results, drawings, etc. that support and amplify statements made in the previous compartments. It is usually titled *Attachments* or *Appendices*.

Plan for a Formal Proposal

Formal proposals are normally lengthy documents, which sometimes run to several volumes. Most formal proposals are written in response to a Request for Proposal (RFP) issued by the government or a large commercial organization. Often, the RFP stipulates the major topics each proposing company must address, the sequence in which the information must be presented, and sometimes, the maximum number of words for each section. Although there is some similarity between the formats stipulated by the different agencies issuing RFPs, there are sufficient variations to make it impossible to present a "standard" outline here. The sections listed below are a composite of several outlines.

The major compartments of a formal proposal are illustrated in Figure 5–6. When the compartments are converted to headings, the outline looks like this:

Letter of Transmittal (optional)
Cover
Title Page
Summary

Figure 5-6 Typical writing plan for a formal proposal

Summary	A synopsis of the proposal's main features, including the total cost
Introduction	The purpose, background to, and scope of the proposal
Proposal Details	A detailed description of the problem and what needs to be done
Experience	The proposer's experience and capability to handle the project
Evidence	Appendices supporting the proposal: charts, cost analyses, statistics, drawings
The Problem	The proposer's understanding of the problem and what must be achieved
The Approach	How the proposer will undertake the project and resolve the problem
Org. and Planning	A detailed description of how the project will be managed
Exceptions	Variances from the RFP: the reason and how they will be handled
Price Proposal	A detailed analysis of the cost of implementing the proposal

Table of Contents
Introduction
The Problem (Description of Problem or Situation)
The Approach (Approach to Resolving the Problem or Improving the Situation)
Organization and Planning
Exceptions
Price Proposal
Experience:
    Company
    Employees
Evidence (Appendices)

Letter of Transmittal

When attached to a formal proposal, a letter of transmittal assumes much greater importance than the standard cover letter attached to the front of a semiformal or formal report. Normally signed by an executive of the proposing company, it comments on the most significant aspects of the proposal and sometimes the cost. It is similar to the Executive Summary for a long report.

Summary

The Summary mentions the purpose of the proposal, touches briefly on its highlights, and states the total cost. If an Executive Summary is bound inside the proposal, the Summary is often omitted.

Introduction

As in a report, the Introduction describes the background, purpose, and scope of the proposal. If the proposal is prepared in response to an RFP, it refers to the RFP and the specific terms of reference or requirements stipulated by the originating authority.

Description of Problem or Situation

This section describes the problem that needs to be resolved or the situation that needs to be improved. It usually includes

- a statement of the problem or situation, as defined by the RFP,
- an elaboration of the problem or situation and its implications (to demonstrate the proposer's full understanding of the circumstances), and
- the proposer's understanding of any constraints or special requirements.

Approach to Resolving Problem or Improving Situation

The proposer describes how the company will tackle the problem or situation and states specifically *what* will be done, *why* it will be done, and, in broad terms, *how* it will be done. As this is the proposer's solution to the problem or method for resolving the situation, this section must be written in strong, definite, convincing terms, which will give the reader confidence that the proposing company knows how to undertake the task.

Organization and Planning

Here, the "how" of the Approach section is expanded to show exactly what steps the proposer will take.

- Under *Organization,* the proposer describes how a project group will be established, its composition, its relationship to other components of the proposing company, and how it will interface with the client's organization.
- Under *Planning,* the proposer outlines a complete project plan and, for each stage or aspect, exactly what steps will be taken and what will be achieved or accomplished.

Exceptions

Sometimes a company may conceive an unusual approach that not only solves the problem but also offers significant advantages, yet deviates from one or more of the client's specified requirements. These exceptions are listed and the reason why each need not be met is clearly explained.

Price Proposal

The proposer's price for the project is stated as an overall price and then broken down into schedules for each phase of the project. The extent and method of pricing is usually specified by the RFP.

This section of the proposal may be placed in various positions. The RFP may stipulate that it appear at the front; here, as an attachment; or even as a separate document.

Experience

The proposing company describes its overall experience and history and its particular experience in resolving problems or handling situations similar to those described in the RFP. It details the key persons who will be assigned to the project and describes their experience in a curriculum vitae.

Appendices

The appendices contain supporting documents, specifications, large drawings and flow charts, schedules, equipment lists, etc. — all of which are referenced in the proposal.

CHAPTER 6

Customizing Letters, Reports, and Proposals

So far we've talked about how to organize and structure your information into logical and easy-to-understand documents. In this chapter we are going to suggest additional ways for you to write and present your information so it is appealing to read, easy to retrieve, adaptable to other cultures, and acceptable to both genders. You have only one chance, in writing, to make your impression. You need to make sure it is the impression you intend.

Using Information Design to Draw Attention

You can help your readers understand and access information through the appearance of your documents. We call this **Information Design**. The suggestions we provide here will help your information "jump off the page" and make it easier to read and understand. The content and structure of your document is still important, but using Information Design techniques will enhance its readability.

Computerized word processing makes it much easier to incorporate Information Design techniques into all types of documents, such as letters, memos, reports, faxes, and notices.

Insert Headings as Signposts

In longer letters and reports, particularly those discussing several aspects of a situation, you can help your reader find information by inserting headings. Headings serve as an outline of or road map to your information. Each heading must be informative, summarizing clearly what is covered in the paragraphs that follow. If, for instance, we had replaced the heading preceding this paragraph with the single word "Headings," it would not have summarized adequately what this section describes.

NEVER USE ALL CAPITAL LETTERS FOR A HEADING, BECAUSE IT MAKES THE WORDS MORE DIFFICULT TO READ.

Studies show that only 23% of readers actually read titles set in all capital letters. Similarly, underlining also makes the text more difficult to read. Underlines were used when documents were typed on typewriters and writers did not have the options word processors provide. There is no reason to use an underline when word processing packages offer so many other options for emphasizing text. The structure of your headings must, however, be consistent throughout the text. For example, you can use different sizes of the *same* font, set in bold and/or italicized letters:

Level 1 heading (14 point, bold): **Form Strong Sentences**

Level 2 heading (12 point, bold): **Write Emphatic Sentences**

Level 3 heading (12 point, bold, italic): ***Use the Active Voice***

Here are some suggestions for integrating headings into the text.

Centre Main Headings

A main heading should be centred in the middle of the page. This is reserved for major topics, like "Introduction." Set them in large boldface type so they stand out from the rest of the text.

Centre Subsidiary Headings

A subsidiary heading is also positioned in the middle of the page, but does not have the same emphasis as the main heading. Sometimes a subsidiary heading is used as a subtitle to a main heading. Set subsidiary headings in boldface type and in a type that is smaller than the Main Heading's type, but larger than the body text's type.

Side Headings

Side headings introduce a new section of text, are usually set in boldface or italics, or in a larger type size than the body text to show emphasis, and are set flush with the left margin. Paragraphs following a side heading are also set with all lines flush with the left margin. In contemporary writing, the first line of each paragraph is seldom indented.

Subparagraph Headings and Subparagraphing

Subparagraph headings and the text that follows them are indented about five spaces or to a 1-cm tab position. The first line is not indented further. Each subparagraph is typed as a solid block, which helps readers *see* the subordination of ideas. Indenting the entire paragraph is another way of visually helping the reader.

Secondary Subparagraphing

If further subparagraphing is necessary, the headings and subparagraphs are indented a further five spaces or to the next 1-cm tab position (a total of 2 cm) from the left margin. The first line is not indented further.

Headings Built Into a Paragraph   In this arrangement, the text continues immediately after the heading. Paragraph headings like these can be used for main paragraphs, subparagraphs, and secondary subparagraphs. Usually, a paragraph heading applies only to one paragraph of text. The headings can be italic, bold, or both, but never underlined.

Subparagraphing Combined with Paragraph Numbering

If you are numbering your paragraphs and need to integrate headings into the text, as can happen with a long document, manual, or procedure, similar rules apply:

1. Side Headings

1.1 When paragraph numbers are used, side headings normally are assigned simple consecutive paragraph numbers, as has been done here.

1.2 Where only one paragraph follows a side heading, it is not assigned a separate paragraph number and is typed with its left margin flush with the side heading, as has been done in the paragraph immediately below heading 1.3.

1.3 Subparagraph Headings and Subparagraphing

If more than one paragraph follows a subparagraph heading, each is assigned an identification number or letter:

a) This would be the first subparagraph.

b) This would be the second subparagraph.

c) Each subparagraph can be further subdivided into a series of very short secondary subparagraphs:

   (1) Here is a secondary subparagraph.

   (2) Ideally, each secondary subparagraph should contain no more than one sentence.

d) **Inserting a Heading**   Secondary subparagraphs may also be assigned subparagraph headings.

Choose Only One Font

A font, such as Century Schoolbook or Arial, is a set of characters with the same features. Fonts are divided into *serif* (they have a slight finishing stroke: T) and **sans serif** (they don't have a finishing stroke: T). The font you choose will project an image of you, your company, and your document:

- Statistics show that serif fonts, like Century Schoolbook and Times New Roman, are easier to read on paper because the finishing stroke of each letter leads the reader's eye to the next letter. Consequently, serif fonts should be used for longer documents. For example, this text is printed in Sabon.

- Sans serif fonts, like Arial or Century Gothic, are clean, clear, and portray a neat and modern image, yet are not as easy to read on paper and are only suitable for shorter paper documents. However, sans serif fonts are easier to read onscreen and should be used for email messages.

Once you decide on a font, you should stay with it. Don't use a different font to show emphasis. Rather, use **boldface**, *italics,* or a larger point size to emphasize your text. (Letterheads and logos are excluded from this guideline: often the font in a letterhead will not be the same as the document font.)

Make sure that the character size you choose is appropriate for your document and audience. In a one-page letter or memo you may use a 10-point size to help keep the document to only one page. In a longer document, use a 12-point size: the type will be slightly larger and the reader's eyes won't tire as easily as with a smaller point size. If you know your audience is older, use a larger point size — at least 12 points — so it is easier to read.

Justify Only on the Left

Word processors make it easy to justify both the left and right margins, which means all lines begin and end at exactly the same place on both sides of the page. We recommend you justify only the text on the left and leave the right side "ragged"; otherwise the computer will automatically increase the size of the spaces between words and characters to force the right margin to be straight. These spaces will make the words either too crowded or too far apart, which is stressful for readers' eyes, because they constantly have to adjust to the uneven spacing. It may seem only a subtle difference, yet it's something you can control to make reading more pleasant. This paragraph is set "ragged right."

Use Margins to Draw Attention

Many people hesitate to change the standard settings that come with word processing packages. Yet once they see the value of being unique, they are easily convinced to try a new way. Try using a left-hand column for headings (about 1/3 of the page), and a right-hand column for the text. This helps draw readers' eyes and attention to the headings so they can retrieve information faster.

Figure 6–1 shows two proposals. One, (a), is presented in the conventional format with the text justified to the left margin, while the other, (b), is presented with a left-hand margin for headings and a right-hand margin for text. The latter takes up more space, but makes the information much more accessible. Turn to Mavis Hamilton's proposal in Figure 5–4 for an example.

Use White Space to Break Up Text

Adding white space or areas without text is another valuable Information Design technique. You can also use diagrams and figures to break up long passages of text and to complement the message. A simple flow chart or table makes a nice diversion for the reader and presents the information in a more visual and concrete way.

Tell your message with pictures whenever you can. For example, if you write an incident report describing an accident in which you were involved, you could spend paragraphs describing in detail the positions of the vehicles prior to, during, and after the accident. Or you could sketch a neat diagram and attach it to the report.

Figure 6-1   Two different ways to present headings

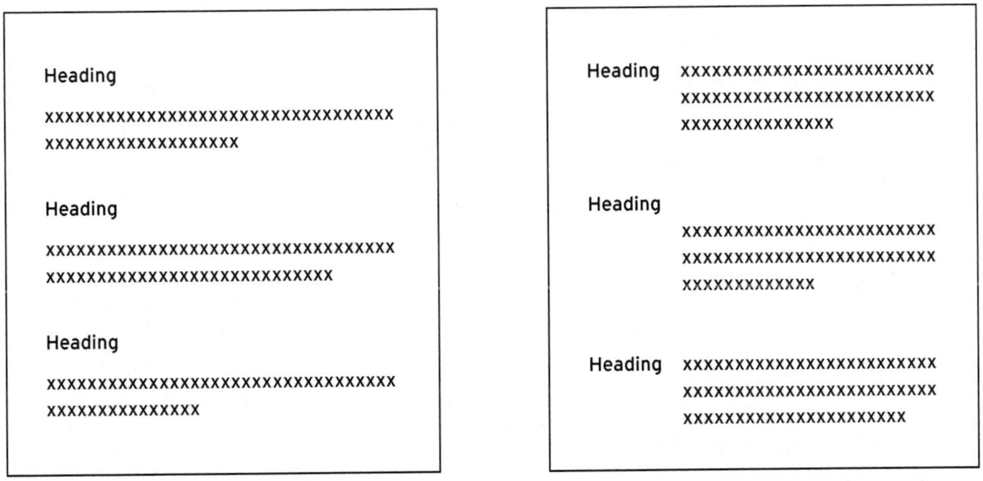

(a) Conventional margins and headings

(b) Wider margins and left-justified headings

Use Lists to Break Up Information

The appearance of your paragraphs may make your readers less receptive to your information. Lists or subparagraphs can help break up text and make it visually more acceptable. Here is an excerpt from a report written without Information Design:

> Opening a service office in Red Deer, Alberta will help us to be more responsive as a service provider to the Red Deer business community. We will be able to meet customers' requests for service much more quickly. On average, response time will be cut by 1 1/2 hours, compared to the current travel time from either our Calgary or Edmonton offices. In addition, we will reduce travel costs. Because service time is charged at a standard hourly rate, we currently bear all travel costs. Having service representatives come from a local office will reduce these travel costs to an almost negligible amount. Third, we will be able to increase our company's visibility to the Red Deer business community. Sales representatives report they currently have difficulty convincing potential clients that we can respond rapidly to urgent demands for service. A *local* service office will put an end to this fear.

A reader facing a long paragraph like this will subconsciously expect it to be "heavy going," and so will start reading it unenthusiastically, almost with a negative attitude to your information. This makes it much harder for you, as a writer, to encourage your readers to accept your ideas. You can avoid this resistance if you separate the information into smaller chunks, in effect forming a list.

If we break up the second sentence by adding a colon after *We will be able to*, and then make a numbered or bulleted list of the suggestions that follow, the information is much easier to read and understand. Watch what happens visually:

> Opening a service office in Red Deer, Alberta will help us to be more responsive as a service provider to the Red Deer business community. We will be able to:
>
> - meet customers' requests for service much more quickly. On average, response time will be cut by 1 1/2 hours compared to the current travel time from either our Calgary or Edmonton offices.
>
> - reduce travel costs. Because service time is charged at a standard hourly rate, we currently bear all travel costs. Having service representatives come from a local office will reduce these travel costs to an almost negligible amount.
>
> - increase our company's visibility to the Red Deer business community. Sales representatives report they currently have difficulty convincing potential clients that we can respond rapidly to urgent demands for service. A *local* service office will put an end to this fear.

These three subparagraphs contain the same information as the initial non-stop paragraph. But this time, the information does not appear nearly as forbidding. In fact, readers know, before they read a word, they are going to be presented with three ideas.

Use Tables for Text

Using tables to display information can also help you design your information for maximum impact. Many people reserve tables for numerical data; we suggest using them to present text in an easily accessible format that compartmentalizes the information. Figure 6–2 shows a table designed to describe the writing compartments for a request letter.

Use Columns to Increase Readability

Although columns are not suitable for correspondence, they certainly can be used for reports or in an attachment to a letter. The value of using columns is described in Figure 6–3.

Writing for an International Audience

As we grow into a more global economy, we must pay even more attention to identifying who we are writing to, and to tailoring the message to that person. Often this means learning a different set of rules for communicating with new customers and business associates.

You need to be sensitive to the idea that in many cultures starting with a Summary Statement (getting right down to business) may be considered rude.

Figure 6-2   Using a table to present text

Writing Plan for a Request	
Compartment	**Contents**
Summary	A brief description of your request and a stated request for approval
Background or Reason	The circumstances leading up to the request
Request Details	A detailed explanation of what your request includes, what will be gained if the request is approved, any problems the request may cause, and what the cost will be
Action	A statement that identifies clearly what you want the reader to do after reading your request

Figure 6-3   The benefits to be gained by displaying text in columns

---

Setting Text in Two Columns Increases Readability

Using a newspaper-style, two-column printed text area helps guide the reader. The line length is forced to be shorter so a reader's eye can follow the line easily and therefore is less stressed. Imagine how difficult it would be to read a newspaper that was printed in one long six-inch-wide column!

We don't recommend this format for letters or short reports, but it can have a good impact on newsletters, longer reports, and technical proposals.

This column format is especially useful when you insert graphics into a document. Text and graphics can be clearly integrated by "wrapping" text around the image. The two are then visually linked.

Graphics that are used in a two-column format also help to balance the page. Often a graphic is inserted and seems to be isolated because there is too much white space around it. With two columns, one column offsets the other.

Another benefit of the two-column format is that it forces the author to write shorter paragraphs; otherwise, the column would be a big block of text without any breaks.

Writing Business Correspondence

Often, business people (especially North Americans) try explaining that they start with the most important information right away because it's more efficient to put the main message up front. However, we must remember the many other cultures that have their own centuries-old traditions of communication, and recognize that *we* have to adapt our own methods of communication to suit them. As our world becomes smaller with world-wide communication, writers must understand the culture prevalent in each society they write to and make adjustments in their writing so they do not offend their readers.

In adjusting your writing, though, you do not need to entirely discard the Pyramid Method. You can still use the pyramid for the central part of your message, but you need to precede it with a personal greeting and polite remarks concerning the health and happiness of your reader and, often, of your reader's family. You will also need to end your message with a polite closing remark, such as wishing the reader continuing good health and prosperity in the months and years ahead. Figure 6–4 shows how to construct letters for readers beyond the Western world.

This adaptation is appropriate for readers you have previously corresponded with. However, to new or more traditional readers, placing the Summary Statement so close to the greeting may still seem too abrupt. For these audiences, move the Summary Statement further down in the correspondence. The revised writing pyramid looks like this:

1. Greeting
2. Background
3. Details
4. Outcome and Summary Statement (combined)
5. Complimentary Close

These revised writing pyramids apply not only to formal business letters but also to memos and electronic means of communication, such as faxes and email.

Some Writing Guidelines

Changing the order of information is not the only part of a message that requires attention. When you write in English to readers whose first language is not English (for example, German, French, Italian, Spanish, Malay, or Cantonese) you need to choose

Figure 6-4 Adapted writing pyramid for a letter to non-Western readers

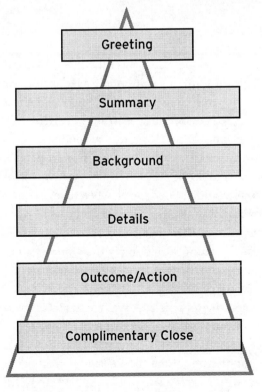

- Gives a personal message mentioning past mutual association and enquiring after the correspondent's health

- States what you most want the reader to know or hear

- Describes the circumstances leading up to the communication

- Gives a detailed description of the occurrence or information

- States the result, or what action is being or will be taken, including what is being requested of the reader

- Gives a pleasant message wishing your reader and his or her family and associates well, and wishing for both your continued pleasant mutual association

words that will be clearly understood. This also holds true for other English-speaking cultures. In the United Kingdom, for instance, the word "fortnight," meaning "two weeks," is commonly used, yet in the United States, and even in parts of Canada, it would not be understood. Similarly, the word "presently" has different meanings in the U.S. and the U.K. Here are some guidelines:

- Avoid long, complex words. If you have a choice between two or more words or expressions that have roughly the same meaning, choose the simpler of the two. For example, write "pay" rather than "salary" or "remuneration."

- Use the same word to describe the same action or product consistently throughout your document. Decide, for example, whether you will refer to money in the bank as *funds, currency, deposits,* or *money.* We often use the word "capital" to refer to money, yet we should avoid using it when writing to international audiences since it may be misinterpreted as a reference to a city (capitol), or to mean "That's ideal!"

- Always use a word in the same sense. You could confuse a non-English-speaking reader if you were to write in one sentence, "It would not be *appropriate* to transfer funds from Account A to Account B" (meaning it would not be suitable to do so), and then in another, "We had insufficient funds to *appropriate* Company A" (meaning to take over or buy out Company A).

Meeting and Speaking

When visiting other countries, it's important you understand and adapt to their local culture and business etiquette. People in Eastern Europe for instance, have major but subtle differences between western and eastern perceptions of good manners and effective communication techniques. For example, it is inappropriate to start a meeting by immediately describing why everyone is there and what they want to accomplish.

At the start of a meeting between North American and Russian business people, members of both companies would sit around a table, be served refreshments, be introduced to each other, and engage in polite conversation about travel, where they live, the weather, and the health of each other's families. Business should *never* be brought up at the start of the meeting. It is also bad manners to pour yourself a second cup of coffee: that is *always* the host's prerogative, because the action would imply that your host has not been hospitable enough. Nothing would be said, but the sudden pause in conversation would tell you that you'd committed a faux pas.

The business discussion would start when the topic is eventually introduced by a member of the host country. Only then should you start describing your plans and ideas, and even then you'll discover it should be done in a roundabout way. Where we are accustomed to putting the main message right up front, using the *tell-tell-tell* method, in some countries it is more customary to start with a brief history of the subject and then lead into the point you want to make. Remember, too, to choose your words carefully, because your hosts may not interpret some words in the same way we do.

Some Cultural Differences

In some cultures, for example, if you were told "It really would not be convenient to pay your hotel expenses by credit card," you might assume that it *could* be done but that it is the *less-preferred* method when, in fact, "It would not be convenient" is really a polite way of saying that it simply *cannot be done* (perhaps because they don't have the facilities for accepting credit cards).

Similarly, in some Pacific Rim countries it is severely impolite to directly contradict a speaker or to say "No" to a suggestion. You should nod your head and say something like: "That is a possibility," or "We will consider that." In Japan this technique is known as Bokashi and has a long cultural history.

In many Eastern European countries business people always wear dark suits and black shoes to a meeting. If you were to wear a grey sports jacket, contrasting dark slacks, and light grey shoes, your choice of dress might be considered a slight against your hosts. In addition, when travelling in Europe, the farther east you go the more frequently people shake hands: always when they first meet each day, and sometimes several times afterward, if they are parted for a time and then rejoin each other.

As world markets expand and boundaries between countries become less apparent, we need to become even more sensitive to the cultural differences that effect how people from other cultures act and react to the way we conduct ourselves, and particularly to the way we present information.

If you are going to be doing business with other nations, visit your local library and research business communication standards in the countries you will be corresponding with or visiting.

Writing Non-Gender-Specific Language

Historically, the traditional view that men were warriors and hunters, and subsequently breadwinners, and women were caregivers, homemakers, and child-rearers, defined gender roles in society.

Today we recognize that women and men have equal rights and can perform equally well in most tasks and occupations. Consequently, we now see, for example, more male secretaries, nurses, and child care workers, and more female airline pilots, engineers, truck drivers, and backhoe operators. Unfortunately, our language hasn't always kept pace with these changes and we still see sexually biased language like the following:

A secretary will be brought in to record the minutes of the executive committee meeting. *She* will also be responsible for making travel arrangements for the meeting participants.

The committee decided to hire an engineer. *He* will evaluate the erosion caused when the river overflowed its banks.

In both cases the writer did not know whether the secretary or the engineer was male or female. They simply *assumed* that the secretary would be female and the engineer would be male because they have been influenced by generations who perpetuated this stereotype. It's necessary to consciously eradicate gender-specific references from our writing until we automatically use non-gender-specific ones. For example,

A secretary will be brought in to write the minutes of the executive committee meeting and to make travel arrangements for the meeting participants.

The committee decided to hire an engineer to evaluate the erosion caused when the river overflowed its banks last summer.

These examples are straightforward and fairly obvious. However, some subtle gender-specific references are more difficult to detect and correct. For example, the script for a recent educational video depicted a 12-year-old boy arriving home from school:

Exterior: Gavin walks up the path, leaps up the steps, and inserts a key into the front door:

Cut to interior: We hear a radio playing. The door opens and Gavin enters. He drops his books on a side table, and calls up the stairs.

GAVIN: "Mom? I'm home!"

The scriptwriter had assumed that it would always be a mother at home. Before shooting the scene the script was changed so that Gavin said:

GAVIN: "Mom? Dad? I'm home!"

Eliminate Generic Masculine Pronouns

When describing managers, supervisors, architects, technicians, accountants and lawyers, our language has historically abounded with masculine pronouns. The engineer described earlier is a typical example. Here is another, this time described in a company's operating procedures:

4.3 Training Coordinator   *His* primary role is to plan, organize, and coordinate all training courses held at DEF company. *He* also is responsible for promoting (advertising) the courses to staff and counselling employees *he* feels should attend.

There are several ways you can remove the male pronouns:

1. Repeat the job title in the description, and abbreviate it:

   4.2 Training Coordinator The primary role of the training coordinator (TC) is to plan, organize, and coordinate all training courses held at DEF company. The TC also is responsible for promoting (advertising) the courses to staff and counselling employees who should attend.

2. Use a bulleted list:

   4.3 Training Coordinator The training coordinator is responsible for
   - planning, organizing, and coordinating all training courses held at DEF company,
   - promoting (advertising) the courses to staff, and
   - counselling employees who should attend.

3. Create a table:

   4.5 Training Coordinator

Primary Responsibility	Secondary Responsibility
To plan, organize, and coordinate all training courses held at DEF company	1. To promote (advertise) courses to staff 2. To counsel employees who should attend

4. Replace the male pronoun with "you" and "your":

   4.5 Training Coordinator *Your* primary role is to plan, organize, and coordinate all training courses held at DEF company. *You* also are responsible for promoting (advertising) the courses to staff and counselling employees *you* feel should attend.

   (*Note:* If you use "you " in one part of a document, be consistent and use it throughout the document. Avoid bouncing back and forth between "you" and "he" or "she.")

5. Replace the male pronoun with "he or she":

   4.6 Training Coordinator The training coordinator's primary role is to plan, organize, and coordinate all training courses held at DEF company. *His or her* responsibilities also include promoting (advertising) the courses to staff and counselling employees *he or she* feels should attend.

   (*Note:* This is the least recommended method.)

6. Change singular pronouns to plural pronouns:

   4.3 Training Coordinator Their primary role is to plan, organize, and coordinate all training courses held at DEF company. *They* also are responsible for promoting (advertising) the courses to staff and counselling employees *they* feel should attend.

   (*Note:* This method can be used only when the description lends itself to using plural nouns and pronouns. It may be interpreted that there is more than one Training Coordinator.)

Replace Gender-Specific Nouns

Each province has its Workers Compensation Board, an organization that provides financial help to employees who are injured at work. Yet, not many years ago, all Workers Compensation Boards in Canada were know as *Workmans* Compensation Boards. The previous title seemed to imply that the Board provided help *only* to male workers, which was not true. Similarly, until about 12 years ago, flight attendants on airlines were known as stewardesses, implying that the job was only held by women. Again, this assumption is plainly inaccurate.

Many other job titles are equally gender-specific and predominantly male-oriented. These have been changed in recent years so that the titles refer to both male and female employees. Table 6–1 lists some gender-specific titles and suggests better alternatives.

The term "man-hours" was previously used to define the time that would be expended on a particular job. Today we write "work-hours" or "staff-hours."

Table 6-1   Alternative and preferred names for gender-specific titles

Instead of	Write	Instead of	Write
actor/actress	actor (for both)	postman	letter/mail carrier
chairman	chairperson/chair	repairman	service technician
cowboy	cattle rancher	salesman	sales representative
fireman	firefighter	spokesman	spokesperson
foreman	supervisor	workman	worker or employee
policeman/woman	police officer	waiter/waitress	server/waiter (for both)
manhours	work-hours/staff-hours		

Be Consistent When Referring to Men and Women

In recent history, men have used the courtesy title *Mr.* to precede their names. Until 20 years ago, women had two courtesy titles, which denoted whether they were married or single: *Mrs.* and *Miss.* Today, a woman's marital status is *never* implied in a professional title: all women should be referred to as *Ms.* (English is not the only language to have used such a system. For example, in France men were traditionally referred to as *Monsieur* and women, generally, as *Madame* or *Mademoiselle,* depending on their age. In Russian, a sex-identifying title is not placed before a person's name, but a woman's family name has an "a" added to the end to denote that the person is female: for example, Boris Serov vs. Svetlana Serova.) When writing to people in other cultures, stick to the English conventions: Mr. or Ms.

And, remember, *never* address a letter to "Dear Sir or Madam"!

CHAPTER 7

The Language of Business Writing

Previous chapters have shown you how to plan and write business communications that convey information quickly and efficiently. The techniques they describe will help you become a well-organized, effective communicator. But the effect can be harmed if you use weak, wishy-washy words, write unemphatic, convoluted sentences, and construct uncoordinated, rambling paragraphs. This chapter will show you how to avoid some of the common language handling pitfalls that can often inadvertently downgrade the effectiveness of your business letters, memos, emails, reports, and proposals.

The Subtle Impact of Good Language

When business manager Dana Courtland receives a well-written business report, she does not consciously notice that its words are well chosen, its sentences are properly formed, and its paragraphs read smoothly and interestingly. The main impression she gains is of a confident, well-thought-out communication that deserves her attention. Conversely, if she receives a letter in which there are vague or misspelled words, incomplete sentences, or inadequately developed paragraphs, she gains the impression of a writer who is careless, unemphatic, and disorganized. By inference, Dana may assume the letter contains only routine or unimportant information.

First we'll discuss paragraphs and show how you can shape them to achieve a coherent, efficient flow of information. Then we'll look at sentences and examine how they can be sharpened to create a strong impact. Third, we'll show you how to choose and use words effectively. Along the way, we'll also look at some structural implications, including how to punctuate sentences and paragraphs, how to use the Pyramid Method to direct readers' attention within a paragraph, and how to use abbreviations and numbers in narrative.

Constructing Coherent Paragraphs

In previous chapters we have used the Pyramid Method to structure email, letters, memos, reports, and proposals. We can also use a scaled down version of the pyramid to design paragraphs. For a paragraph, the Summary Statement is known as the **Topic Sentence** (it's the *main message* the paragraph is conveying), and the supporting details are known as the **Supporting Sentences**, as shown in Figure 7–1.

A paragraph structured using the Pyramid Method is easy to read:

> *The meeting achieved only one of its three objectives.* **The committee approved a $6000 budget increase for the Beta project, but deferred approval of the proposed seven-week extension to the Arbutus program until Mr. Copthorne has submitted a progress report. The committee also decided to delay approving the request for six additional hirings until the project group leaders provide detailed job descriptions.**

The topic sentence (in italics) is always a general overview that sums up the main points. The remaining sentences then provide details. And sometimes there is a final sentence that draws a **Miniconclusion** or points the way ahead; as in this second paragraph:

Figure 7-1   The pyramid writing plan applied to the paragraph

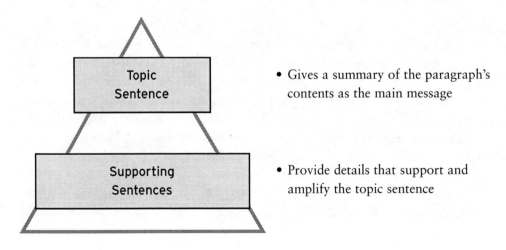

Topic Sentence
- Gives a summary of the paragraph's contents as the main message

Supporting Sentences
- Provide details that support and amplify the topic sentence

Topic Sentence	The Human Resources Department says that 30% of the job applications we receive are rejected because of careless preparation. They cite four main causes: failure to answer all of the questions on
Supporting Sentences	the form, messy handwriting, answers which do not address the questions, and one-sentence answers when a paragraph-form answer is clearly called for. The HR staff claims that the care an
Miniconclusion	applicant takes in completing the form is an indicator of an applicant's potential as a quality employee.

Technically; a topic sentence can be placed at the beginning, in the middle, or at the end of a paragraph; or it can even be implied. But for most business writing we recommend placing topic sentences right up front, so readers learn *immediately* what the paragraph is about. Just occasionally, to gain particular emphasis, they may be placed at the end of a paragraph, where they act like an exclamation mark:

> We wanted to know what had caused our customers to buy the product. We were interested in whether any, and if so which, media advertising had influenced their decisions. We wondered where they would normally expect to buy such a product and whether they were successful on their first attempt. And we were keen to identify their age groups and professional or employment status. *Clearly, we needed more than just a simple questionnaire.*

Develop Good Information Flow

To be effective, a paragraph must carry a reader smoothly from its opening sentence to its closing sentence and must impress a reader with the logic of its development. This means searching for a general narrative pattern, which in most cases is

- chronological order,
- cause to effect, or
- evidence to conclusion.

These patterns are not meant to be so rigid that they inhibit how you write. For example, the 'meetings' paragraph quoted on page 118 is in chronological order, the "application forms" paragraph above progresses generally from cause to effect; and the "questionnaire" paragraph is arranged from evidence to conclusion. The importance of finding a pattern and adhering to it becomes apparent in the following two paragraphs:

An incoherent paragraph with poor continuity	The memory loss occurred when an unauthorized operator removed the CD-ROM disk from the drive. It was on an adjacent table and a heavy parcel was dropped on it. The regular operator had extracted only 20% of the Beta file from it. The unauthorized operator needed access to a different CD-ROM, removed the disk

containing the Beta file, and placed it on the table rather than in its protective sleeve. A mail clerk then dropped the parcel, which apparently had been resting on a gritty surface, onto it. All this happened while the regular operator was on her lunch break. The grit scratched the disk, inhibiting access to the stored information.

A coherent paragraph with good continuity (chronological sequence)

The memory loss occurred when an unauthorized operator removed a CD-ROM disk from the drive. The regular operator had extracted about 20% of the Beta file from the disk when she stopped for lunch. During her absence, another operator who needed access to a different CD-ROM disk removed her disk from the drive and placed it on an adjacent table rather than into its protective sleeve. Shortly after, a mail clerk dropped a heavy parcel, which apparently had been resting on a gritty surface, on top of the disk. The grit scratched the disk, inhibiting access to the stored information.

Within each paragraph there also needs to be continuity between the sentences, to build bridges as the reader progresses from one thought to the next. This paragraph is choppy because it is composed of a series of separate thoughts:

Poor Continuity

The supervisors resented being told they had to join the union. They knew they were part of management. They had checked that the same rule did not apply in other companies. They were annoyed their opinion had not been solicited. They asked to meet with the company president.

This paragraph is smoother because it refers to previous expressions and repeats key words ("As supervisors they," "They had also," "And they were," and "So they prepared...."):

Better Continuity

The supervisors resented being told they had to join the union. As supervisors, they knew that they were traditionally part of management. They had also checked with supervisors at other companies and found the rule did not apply there. And they were annoyed that management had not even asked for their opinion. So they prepared a brief requesting a meeting with the company president.

Parallelism also plays an important role in building paragraph rhythm, just as it does in building sentence rhythm. In a paragraph that is internally parallel the verbs (and sometimes the adverbs, nouns, and adjectives) have a similar form: a form the reader readily recognizes as rhythm. For example, two expressions are repeated in the paragraph below ("Perhaps...and...," and "Or you..."), which makes readers feel comfortable as they progress through the stages described in the paragraph.

There are various occasions when you will need to present information to a small audience. Perhaps you will attend a seminar or equipment demonstration and, on your return, you will be expected to brief other members of your department. Or you may develop a new process or procedure and have to describe its advantages to other department supervisors. Perhaps visitors will tour your offices and you will be asked to brief them on the work you do. Or you may visit a government department where you have to make a sales pitch for a zoning adjustment. Whatever the circumstances, you will be selling ideas.

These are only brief examples of the many ways you can develop skill in creating continuity within the paragraphs you write. To find more information, refer to one of the many handbooks of English usage available from libraries and bookstores in your area.

Make Subparagraphs Work for You

Subparagraphing is an excellent way to help readers *see* how you are grouping or separating your ideas (see "Use Lists to Break Up Information" on page 108). Here are some tips to help you write good subparagraphs:

- Let the reader see how you are subordinating ideas by indenting the whole subparagraph as a complete block of information, as is being done here. Don't let subsequent lines run back under the paragraph number, bullet, or heading. If you use sub-subparagraphs, indent them as a complete unit too.

- Either number the subparagraphs or use bullets, as is being done here. Use numbers if you are providing information in a sequence, want to show the priority of the ideas, or will refer to the subparagraph later in the document. At all other times, use bullets.

- If a subparagraph contains more than one sentence, write it "pyramid-style": start with a topic sentence and then let subsequent sentences provide amplification (see how this has been done in the two previous bulleted subparagraphs).

- Always insert an introductory sentence to lead into the subparagraphs (we call this a "lead-in line"). Don't insert a heading and then immediately start with bullets or numbers.

Punctuate your lead-in line and subsequent subparagraphs like this:

- If the lead-in line is a complete sentence, follow it with a colon, start each subparagraph with a capital letter, and close the subparagraph with a period:

  When ordering supplies, follow these steps:

  1. Pull down the dialog box **Placing an Order.**

  2. Click on **Form 2820.**

  3. Type in the requisition number at the top left.

4. Insert the quantity required and a full description of each item.

5. Click on the appropriate **Delivery Instructions** entry.

6. **Save** the order form.

7. Email the order form to central supply.

- If the lead-in line is not a complete sentence, *do not* follow it with a colon (leave it open). Start each subparagraph with a *lower-case* letter and close the subparagraph with a comma (except the last subparagraph, which must close with a period). Insert the word "and" after the comma at the end of the second-last subparagraph. Here is an example:

When ordering supplies

1. pull down the dialog box **Placing an Order**,

2. click on **Form 2820**,

3. type in the requisition number at the top left,

4. insert the quantity required and a full description for each item,

5. click on the appropriate **Delivery Instructions** entry,

6. **Save** the order form, and

7. email the order form to central supply.

(Note: item 6 starts with a capital letter because the first word is a title on the computer screen.)

- When using the "closed" style of lead-in line (with a colon at the end), your subparagraphs may contain more than one sentence. However, when using the "open" style of lead-in line (no colon at the end), your subparagraphs cannot contain more than one sentence, because they are really all part of one long sentence shown as a series of steps.

Forming Strong Sentences

Sentences have dual characteristics: each must be able to stand alone as a complete entity, yet each normally forms part of a larger unit — the paragraph — in which it plays a particular role. A sentence is a writer's front line conveyor of information; and it has to be constructed carefully if it is to contribute properly to a paragraph.

Write Emphatic Sentences

There are two ways you can write the following piece of information:

A.   **The conference record was erased accidentally by Paul Winslett.**

B.   **Paul Winslett accidentally erased the conference record.**

As both sentences contain exactly the same information, we can argue for a long time over which is the better way to present these particular facts. Many people prefer sentence A, because it is more general and does not try to pin the blame so pointedly on Paul. Practical business people, however, prefer sentence B, because they like its directness.

Use the Active Voice

In business, it is much better to be direct by using a simple subject–verb–object construction that describes "who did what":

	Subject (who or what)	Verb (did)	Object (what)
1.	The accountant	completed	the audit.
2.	Emily	calculated	the expenses.
3.	A power outage	shut down	production.
4.	The staff	presented	a farewell gift to Kim Tsung.

This direct form of writing is known as the **active voice**, because it actively conveys information. Sentence B, above, is written in the active voice.

In contrast, sentence A is written in the **passive voice**, because it provides information only passively. We can see its blandness if we convert the four previous sentences into the "what was done by whom" style of the passive voice.

1.   **The audit has been completed by the accountant.**

2.   **The expenses were calculated by Emily.**

3.   **Production was shut down by a power outage.**

4.   **A farewell gift was presented to Kim Tsung by the staff.**

Notice the word "by" in each of these sentences: it can be a signal that you are writing in the passive voice (it shows that something is being done *by* someone). The word "by" does not appear in the four active voice sentences.

Comparing two paragraphs, one constructed mainly of passive voice sentences and one constructed mainly of active voice sentences, clearly demonstrates the difference:

Passive Voice	It was estimated by Jack Herzing that the project will last 15 months. During the initial four months, designs are to be submitted by the architect for approval by Ms. Simpson. A further nine months will be required by the construction company before the new building can be occupied by the mainframe installers. And then it will take two more months for an internal layout plan and an occupation schedule to be prepared by the phase-in team.
Active Voice	Jack Herzing estimated the project will last 15 months. The architects will submit designs for Ms. Simpson to approve during the first four months. The construction company will require nine months, after which the mainframe installers will begin work. The phase-in team will then require two months to plan the internal layout and prepare an occupation schedule.

The active voice offers two immediate advantages: it is shorter (in the above example, 57 words compared with 77 words for the passive voice), and its verbs are much more emphatic:

Passive voice	Active voice
it was estimated by Jack Herzing...	Jack Herzing estimated...
designs are to be submitted by...	the architects will submit...
for approval by Ms. Simpson...	for Ms. Simpson to approve...
will be required by the construction company...	the construction company will require...
can be occupied by the equipment installers...	the equipment installers will move in...
to be prepared by the phase-in team...	the phase-in team will prepare...

These active voice "action" verbs make a writer seem much more confident and, by inference, more competent.

We are not implying you have to use the active voice all the time. To write in the active voice means naming who or what performed the action:

Dana Rooke submitted a three-page proposal.

Head office transferred Harvey Wahl to the Regina branch.

Management hired two summer students to work from May to August.

But, if you do not know or prefer not to name the person or group performing the action, then you have to write in the passive voice:

> The shipment of spare parts for Acme Industries has been lost.

You could write,

> Someone lost the shipment of spare parts destined for Acme Industries,

but that seems to place unnecessary emphasis on an unknown entity: *Someone*.

Alternatively try to identify a "doer" (someone or something) you can name as the subject performing the action:

Rather than write	Try writing
Five cars have been vandalized in the parking lot.	Vandals damaged five cars in the parking lot.
The capital purchases budget has been cut by $86 000.	The controller has cut the capital budget by $86 000.
The printer was left running all weekend.	An operator left the printer running all weekend.

Remember: the active voice creates a much stronger, more emphatic impression than the passive voice.

You can test your "comfortableness" with writing in the active voice by trying Exercise 7–1 and checking your answers against those on page 147.

Write in the First Person

If you were taught not to start a letter with the pronoun "I," you are probably writing letters and reports in an unnaturally roundabout way. When writing email, memos, and business letters (in which you clearly write from one person to another), and in most informal and even some semiformal reports, we recommend using the first person. Using "I" will help you write more easily and more directly. Or, if you feel uncomfortable writing "I" when reporting for your company, then you can write "we" and be just as direct and emphatic. For example,

Using the personal pronouns "I" or "we"	Avoiding the personal pronouns "I" or "we"
I checked the files and found two discrepancies.	The files were checked and two discrepancies were found.
I have ordered a site license for the *4Tell* software program.	A site license has been ordered for the *4Tell* software program.
We have examined our records and can identify only the first of the two invoices you listed.	Our records have been examined and only the first of the two invoices you listed has been identified.

Did you notice that the words "by someone" are implied in each of the sentences in the right-hand column?:

The files were checked [*by someone*] and...

A site license has been ordered [*by someone*] for...

Our records have been examined [*by someone*] and...

This shows the sentences are written in the passive voice (although it is hidden, they still contain the identifier "by").

As a general guideline, use "I" when writing email, memos, letters, and reports in which you present your opinions or describe what you have done. Use "we" when writ-

---

Exercise 7-1

Changing passive voice to active voice

Improve the effectiveness of these sentences, primarily by changing them from the passive voice to the active voice.

1. The meeting was adjourned by the chairperson at 4:30 p.m.

2. At Viking Insurance, the manually operated telephone switching system has been replaced by an automated answering system.

3. At its October meeting, it was agreed by the executive of the company's social club that the Christmas Party should be held on December 16.

4. The product analysis report written by Mavis Barnes was edited by Vic Darwin and illustrated by Rachel Gagné.

5. When Vancourt Business Systems was audited by Revenue Canada, a $30 000 discrepancy was found between reported and actual income.

6. It is recommended that the Westport Travel Insurance Program be adopted.

7. Work was stopped at 1:55 p.m. by a power outage which lasted 4 hours. At 2:30 p.m. it was decided by the office manager that all employees should go home for the remainder of the day.

8. It was decided by the staff development committee that the request from Terry Rozak for attendance at the April Canadian Business Society meeting should be approved.

9. Although a 17% production loss had been predicted by the Steering Committee for the month of August, the actual production loss reported by Production Control was only 6%.

10. It is of some concern to me that a similar interface problem to the one identified by our I.T. department has been faced by your company.

Turn to page 147 for suggested answers.

ing letters and reports that represent your company's views, or when writing memos, reports, and proposals, or when you are writing on behalf of a group of people.

In Chapters 2 and 3 the first person singular ("I") is used frequently throughout the sample emails, letters, and short reports. Even Wendy Riverton's evaluation report in Chapter 4 (pages 71 to 76) uses "I" and "my" almost entirely. She uses "we" and "our" only when referring to the company's policy toward alternative employment methods. But in her proposal to Pacific Restaurants Limited (Chapter 5, pages 93 to 96), Mavis Hamilton uses "we" and "our" exclusively, because she is proposing services that her company, Floral West Imports Ltd., will supply.

Position Words for Maximum Effect

The first and last words in a sentence have the potential to create particular emphasis, *providing effective words are placed there*. Too often, however, these high-impact positions are stolen by unimportant words or expressions that reduce the effectiveness of the sentence. For example,

> **For your information, throughout December our Discount Centre showroom will remain open until 9 p.m. every weekday.**

If we remove the redundant expression "For your information," and rearrange the remaining words so that key words occupy the high-impact positions, the sentence becomes much stronger:

> **Throughout December our Discount Centre showroom will remain open weekdays until 9 p.m.**

Especially check that conditional words and phrases such as *without doubt, however, at least, such matters as,* and *without exception* do not sneak into these positions because they particularly reduce emphasis:

Instead of   The January meeting has been cancelled, *however.*

Write   The January meeting, *however,* has been cancelled.

Instead of   *Without exception,* forward transaction summaries to the Accounts Section by 3 p.m. daily *at the latest.*

Write   Forward transaction summaries to the Accounts Section daily, by no later than 3 p.m.

Instead of   *Be sure to* empty the IN tray once every hour, *at least.*

Write   Empty the IN tray *at least* once every hour.

Write Structurally Sound Sentences

A structurally unsound sentence can disturb readers, who will be vaguely aware that something is not quite right, even if they do not recognize the reason for it. This, in turn, can deflect their attention from the point you are trying to make. The remedy is to make every sentence work for you by keeping it simple, ensuring it has rhythm, and checking it is complete.

Develop Only One Thought

A sentence like the one below will force a reader to stumble and go back over the words to find out what its writer is trying to say:

> There has been a documentation problem in calculating project costs, which possibility was brought to the committee's attention by Ms. Smythe on May 18, but at this time it was considered unimportant, because Mr. Cordon claimed it would not seriously affect the schedule, and now will result in a three-day delay before we can meet with the client to discuss progress payments.

Readers will have trouble because its writer has forgotten the cardinal rule of sentence writing: **Develop only one thought in each sentence.** Although a sentence can have several subordinate clauses, they all must evolve from or support a single thought. To make the above sentence coherent, it needs to be divided into at least two sentences, each developing a *separate* thought:

Sentence 1   There has been a documentation problem in calculating project costs, which will result in a three-day delay before we can meet with the client to discuss progress payments.

Central thought   *There will be a delay.*

Sentence 2   This possibility was predicted by Ms. Smythe at the May 18 meeting, but was considered to be unimportant because Mr. Cordon claimed it would not seriously affect the schedule.

Central thought   *The problem was predicted but ignored.*

The original sentence also violated a useful guideline concerning sentence length: we suggest that, on average, a sentence should not exceed 25–30 words. (The original, long sentence contained 63 words; the two revised sentences each contain 29 words.) However, this guideline can be affected by the complexity of the topic and your knowledge of the reader:

- If a sentence is describing a very general topic for a knowledgeable reader, it can be as long as the 29-word sentences above, or even a little longer.

- If the topic is complex, or if you suspect the reader may have difficulty understanding it, then on average the sentences should be no longer than 15–20 words.

Write Complete Sentences

Every day we see examples of incomplete sentences: on television, in magazines, and especially in advertising. Their writers use them to create a crisp, intentionally choppy effect, which serves their purpose well for the audience they are trying to reach.

Sheer Comfort!

8200 metres high. Wide seats, just like in your living room. Tempting meals when *you* ask for them. Complimentary refreshments. Only on Remick Airlines. Our Business Class. Try us!

If we do the same in our business letters and reports, our sentences are likely to be read with raised eyebrows.

A common and very easy error to make, particularly when your writing is going well and you do not want to interrupt your enthusiasm, is to inadvertently form a **sentence fragment**. For example,

- *The meeting achieved its objective. Even though three members were absent.*

- *The operators were encouraged to leave at 3 p.m. Being the hottest day of the year.*

The first sentence in each example is complete: each has a subject-verb-object construction. But the two second sentences are incomplete because, to be understood, each depends on information contained in the sentence before it.

A useful way to check whether a sentence is complete is to read it aloud as a stand-alone sentence. If it contains a complete thought, it will be understood just as it stands. For example, *The meeting achieved its objective* is a complete thought because you do not need additional information to understand it. So is *The operators were encouraged to leave at 3 p.m.* Yet you cannot say the same when you read the second sentences aloud:

- *Even though three members were absent.*

- *Being the hottest day of the year.*

In most cases a sentence fragment can be corrected by removing the period that separates it from the sentence it depends on, inserting a comma in place of the period, and adding a conjunction or connecting word such as *and, but, which, who,* or *because*:

- The meeting achieved its objective, even though three members were absent.

- The operators were encouraged to leave at 3 p.m., *because it was* the hottest day of the year.

(Note: *Being* has been replaced by *because it was.*)
Here are two more:

- Staff will have to bring lunches or go out for lunch from October 6 to 10. While the lunchroom is being renovated.

  Change the period to a comma

  Staff will have to bring lunches or go out for lunch from October 6 to 10, while the lunchroom is being renovated.

- All 20-year employees are to be presented with a long-service award. Including three who retired earlier in the year.

  Change the period to a comma

  All 20-year employees are to be presented with a long-service award, including three who retired earlier in the year.

In particular, check sentences that start with a word that ends in "–ing" (e.g. *referring, answering, being*) or an expression that ends in "…to" (e.g. *with reference to*):

- With reference to your letter of June 6. We have considered your request and will be sending you a cheque.

  Change the period to a comma

  With reference to your letter of June 6, we have considered your request and will be sending you a cheque.

  Alternatively, you could restructure the sentence (preferred)

  We have considered the request in your letter of June 6 and will be sending you a cheque.

- Referring to the problem of vandalism to employees' automobiles in the parking lot. We will be hiring a security guard to patrol the area from 8 a.m. to 6 p.m., Monday through Friday.

Although the period could be changed to a comma, we recommend restructuring the fragment to form a better sentence:

To resolve the problem of vandalism to employees' automobiles in the parking lot, we will be hiring a security guard....

A similar sentence error occurs if you link two separate thoughts in a single sentence, joining them with only a comma or even no punctuation. The effect can jar a reader uncomfortably:

Marie Shields has been selected for the word processing seminar on May 8, she is not keen to attend.

This awkward construction is known as a **run-on sentence**. It can be corrected by

- replacing the comma with a period to form two complete sentences:

  ...seminar on May 8. She is not keen to attend.

- retaining the comma and following it with *which* or *but*:

  ...seminar on May 8, which she is not keen to attend.

  ...seminar on May 8, but she is not keen to attend.

A run-on sentence with *no* punctuation is even more noticeable:

- The customer claims he has not received an invoice I made up a new one.

Here, either a period or a comma followed by a linking word can be inserted between *invoice* and *I*:

- The customer claims he has not received an invoice, I made up a new one.

- The customer claims he has not received an invoice, so I made up a new one.

It is surprising how easily such simple sentence or punctuation faults can slip by unnoticed — until they reach the reader — who immediately notices them!

To test your punctuation skills, try Exercise 7–2.

Exercise 7-2

Run-on sentences and sentence fragments

Correct any incorrect punctuation you can find in these sentences, particularly punctuation caus-
ing run-on sentences and sentence fragments.

1. The red warning label on the bottle read: "Do not give to children weighing less than 30 kg."
    Definitely not intended for 6-year-olds.

2. I have examined your Nabuchi model 400 Bubble Jet printer, repairs will cost you $88 plus tax.

3. We installed a twelve-line telephone system, right now we need only eight lines. Four lines for
    a planned expansion next year.

4. I am requesting that you transfer my account from your branch at 1620 Portage Avenue to
    your new branch at 310 St. Mary's Road, this confirms my telephone instructions of May 31.

5. With reference to our telephone call regarding leasing a new service van. I have originated a
    purchase order detailing price and delivery dates. To confirm the order.

6. Please book me flights to Toronto on October 16, return on October 20. Aisle seat preferred.

7. Effective June 1, Shirley Watzinger is to be transferred to Accounts Payable, this confirms my
    telephone instructions of yesterday afternoon. Salary and benefits to remain the same.

8. In yesterday's email you described a problem with stationery shipped to you last week.
    Purchase order 2720 Invoice 1514A. Received wet and unusable, I have arranged for Zipper
    Courier to pick it up. Replace with repeat order, ship with same courier.

9. We finished work on the data conversion project March 12. Three days ahead of the scheduled
    completion date, a cause to celebrate!

10. The order from Nesbitt Industries came in by courier at noon on May 27, they had been trying
    to fax us for three days, the fax line was not connected properly

Turn to page 149 for suggested answers.

Keep the Parts Parallel

Just as listeners may not consciously notice rhythm until a musician strikes a discordant
note, readers often do not notice sentence parallelism until they stumble over a non-
parallel sentence. For example,

**The supervisor predicted the problem and was quick in recommending corrective
action.**

We understand what this writer is saying, but the sentence lacks rhythm because its
two verbs (*predicted* and *recommending*) are not in the same form. The expression *quick
in recommending* needs to be changed so that it is parallel with *predicted*. The result is
a much stronger, more definite statement:

The supervisor *predicted* the problem and *quickly recommended* corrective action.

Parallelism becomes especially important when joining two parts of a sentence with a coordinating conjunction such as *and* (as in the above example), *or, but,* a comma, or a correlative such as *either...or; neither...nor;* or *not only...but also.* Here are three examples:

C h a n g e	When the Calgary branch closed, we *transferred* four staff members to other branches and *arrangements were made* for two to retire early.
T o	When the Calgary branch closed, we *transferred* four staff members to other branches and *arranged* for two to retire early.
C h a n g e	You can either *take* the remainder of your vacation time in December or it *can be deferred* until next year.
T o	You can either *take* the remainder of your vacation time in December or *defer* it until next year.
C h a n g e	The project group not only *designed* the program but also was *instrumental in implementing* it.
T o	The project group not only *designed* the program but also *implemented* it.

Parallelism is also important when compiling a list of steps. For example,

When the project is complete, write a project completion report and distribute it as follows:

1. Attach two copies to the contract and mail them to the client.
2. Send one copy, by internal mail, to the accountant, with a request that the final invoice be sent to the client.
3. Place two copies in project file 27-33-18.
4. The final step is to write an email message to each of the branch managers, informing them the report is complete and attach your report to it. The email should state that the report is for information only, and that no action is required on their part.

In steps 2 and 4 (particularly step 4), the verbs are not parallel with those in steps 1 and 3. In step 2, the second part of the sentence (the part that says, "with a request that the final invoice be raised and sent to the client") is not parallel with the first half of the sentence. Revise step 2 like this:

2. Send one copy, by internal mail, to the accountant. Include a note authorizing the accountant to prepare and mail the final invoice.

In step 4, the structure of the whole paragraph is not parallel with the previous steps. Revise it like this:

4. Write an email message to each of the branch managers. State that the project is complete, the report is attached and is for information only, and that no action is required on their part. Attach the report electronically to the email.

Exercise 7-3

Correcting faulty parallelism

Improve the parallelism in the following sentences and short passages.

1. If we buy only three units, the cost will be $187 each, but it will drop to $165 apiece if we buy eight or more units.

2. We selected the model AS800 microprocessor because of its small size, high speed, and because its battery has a 4.5-hour life between charges.

3. A questionnaire was distributed to customers in the Southwood Mall not only to assess the public's reaction but also because it was considered a good method for drawing attention to the new product.

4. The main conclusions drawn from the company's job-sharing experiment show that job sharing
    •   demands supervisors' cooperation,
    •   requires compatible participants,
    •   employee attendance is improved, and
    •   increases individual productivity.

5. When we test-ran the new series of Soapscreen 30-second television commercials before an invited audience, 64% of the general public who viewed them reacted favourably, but of the media specialists who also were invited to attend, only 18% were complimentary.

6. All supervisors are to attend a ten-hour St. John Ambulance course during which they will be given training in administering first aid and how to recognize and helping heart attack victims.

7. On the first day of work, each new employee is to have a medical examination in the morning, and in the afternoon will attend a three-hour company orientation seminar.

8. Jeff Freiberg is to coordinate the project, administration responsibilities have been assigned to Candace Swystun, and a study of the documentation process has been initiated by Hal Kominsky.

9. We have purchased three dozen calculators: 25 model 70s for each assessor at $24.50; 4 model 70s to be held as spare units; and, for the auditors, 2 model Z90s at $38.90 each.

10. The recent downsizing has meant reducing staff by 17 employees, of whom 3 elected early retirement, 4 chose to be transferred to the Brighton office, retraining was chosen by 8 employees, and job-sharing was selected by Millie Yousof and Connie Doucette.

Turn to page 148 for suggested answers.

Notice that parallelism particularly affects the verbs. If you keep the verbs in a sentence in the same form, your sentences are much more likely to have internal parallelism. You can practice doing this in Exercise 7–3, and check your answers against those on page 148.

Choosing the Right Words

The right word used at the right moment and in the right place can create exactly the right effect. But unfortunately we have allowed ourselves to become a generation of lazy word-users: we often use vague, undescriptive, readily available words instead of taking the time to find words that do a much better job. For example,

> **I was held up because I helped some people whose vehicle went into the ditch.**

The vagueness of this sentence plants numerous questions in a reader's mind:

> **How long were you held up?**
>
> **What did you do to help?**
>
> **What vehicle?**
>
> **How did it get into the ditch?**
>
> **Where did this happen?**

Use Words That Paint Pictures

With only a little more effort — just by changing a few words — the sentence could have been much more explicit:

> **I was delayed 40 minutes while I helped pull two passengers from a panel van that had rolled into the ditch 2 km north of Wilman's Corner.**

Look at the changes:

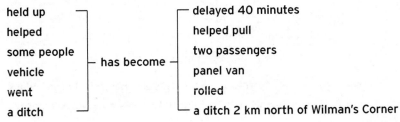

held up		delayed 40 minutes
helped		helped pull
some people	has become	two passengers
vehicle		panel van
went		rolled
a ditch		a ditch 2 km north of Wilman's Corner

The tendency to grab any vague, easy-to-find word rather than to think of a more descriptive word not only can obscure a message, but also may delay communication while the reader contacts the writer to ask questions. As writers it is our responsibility to anticipate what our readers want to know, and then to use clear, descriptive words to provide the facts they need.

So, when you are tempted to write	Pause first and try to think of words such as
contacted communicated with }	emailed, telephoned, talked to, wrote to
put placed }	threw, slid into, rammed, handed, placed dropped, positioned, inserted
got picked up }	bought, were given, borrowed, rented, purchased
went sent }	drove, flew, cycled, walked mailed, emailed, faxed, shipped, air-expressed

The following sentences show how more explicit words improve sentence clarity:

- We *went* to Edmonton. (We *drove...*, We *flew...*)
- The department is *getting* a new copier. (is *buying...*, is *ordering*)
- I *sent* the report yesterday. (I *mailed...*, I *couriered...*, I *delivered...*)
- The proposal has been *put away*. (*...filed.*, *...stored in the library.*)
- When we *communicated* with Mr. Easton, he *put us in the picture* about the problem. (When we *spoke* to Mr. Easton, he *described the paper-feed problem*.)

Use Specifics Rather Than Generalizations

Compare these two month-end progress reports and decide whether Jane or Janet has written the better report:

Jane   The Arbutus program is moving along nicely and should be completed easily by the end of next month.

Janet   The Nova project is 70% complete. Although currently three days behind schedule, it will still be finished by November 30, as planned.

We have found that opinion is often divided, with half of our readers choosing Jane's report and half preferring Janet's.

But what happens if we rephrase the question, like this: "Which one of these two report writers do you think has the better handle on the job?"

This time, over 80% of readers will answer: "Janet!" Why? Because her use of *specifics* persuades them she has everything under control.

Jane's report makes her seem pleasantly but only hazily competent, whereas Janet's makes her sound sure of herself because *she has quoted exact quantities and dates.* Readers are more inclined to believe and have confidence in writers who use strong, definite words and quote exact, rather than vague, information.

Select Short Rather Than Long Words

When searching for descriptive words you have to take care that you do not go to the other extreme and start using large, lesser-used words that can often sound ponderous and pompous rather than clear and specific. An accountant who describes an employee's salary as "remuneration" and the company pension plan as the "superannuation scheme" has allowed this to happen; so has a computer specialist who refers to "sophisticated diagnostic techniques" when he means complex troubleshooting methods, and a manager who describes how her staff has "furthered their competence" when she really means they have gained new skills.

The problem with such overblown words is that they *look* impressive. When you see them in print, you hesitate to tamper with them, as if they were carved in stone.

There are three solid reasons for not using overblown words: your reader may not understand what you have written; you may not fully understand their exact meaning, and so may use them incorrectly (which your reader may notice); and, to your reader, you may seem pompous and overbearing.

Sometimes you will have to use a big word, such as "reverberation," because there is no simpler word you can use as a substitute. At all other times you should choose a simple but exact word that both you and your reader will recognize and understand. Remember the cautionary remarks made by an economy-minded business executive:

> **Never use a 75-cent word when a perfectly sound 30-cent word exists which you can use just as successfully.**

In other words, consider *went* to be a limp, cheap, lustreless, bargain-basement word; *walked* as a sound word at a reasonable price; and *perambulated* as an expensive, gilt-edged word of little real value.

Eliminate Wordy Expressions

We have become so accustomed to seeing other writers use wordy expressions that we tend to think it's all right for us to use them, too. A wordy expression is any word or group of words that, when either removed from or shortened within a sentence, does not change the meaning of the sentence. For example, at first glance these sentences seem properly constructed:

1.   A new office is being built in close proximity to London, Ontario.

2.   The committee was in agreement with Mr. Hanson's proposal.

3.   Ms. Reynaud estimated that the new procedure would result in a $50 000 increase in operating costs annually.

4.   It is our considered opinion that you should make a concerted effort to reduce overhead costs.

Yet each of these sentences would sound more emphatic if the wordy expression(s) it contains are eliminated or shortened:

1.   A new office is being built close to London, Ontario.
     (*in...proximity* has been deleted)

2.   The committee agreed with Mr. Hanson's proposal.
     (*was in agreement with* has been shortened to *agreed*)

3.   Ms. Reynaud estimated that the new procedure would decrease operating costs by $50 000 annually.
     (*result in a* has been deleted)

4.   We believe you should reduce your overhead costs.
     (*It is our considered opinion* has been shortened to *We believe*, and *make a concerted effort to* has been deleted)

The words we have deleted are known as low-information-content (LIC) expressions. When you remove them from a sentence, the sentence contains no less information; in fact, often the sentence is improved. Compare these two examples of the same piece of information:

Wordy
Original

It is a matter of concern that it has been brought to my attention that in the course of the past three months no track has been kept of long distance telephone calls when the Internet is being accessed by I.T. staff. At this point in time you are hereby advised it will be necessary to keep a running record, involving the use of form 2707, of any long distance telephone calls that personnel in the I.T. department make.

With the wordy expressions removed and the remaining words rearranged slightly, the message immediately becomes clear:

Simpler
Revision

I am concerned that for three months I.T. staff have not been recording long-distance telephone calls when they access the Internet. From now on all Internet calls are to be recorded on form 2707.

Table 7–1 contains a list of common wordy expressions. Expressions that you should avoid using are indicated with an X. Alternatives are given for expressions that need to be shortened. Table 7–2 contains a list of clichés or hackneyed expressions that also contribute to wordiness. Exercise 7–4 contains a 10-sentence self-test, to help you identify and remove or shorten clichés and LIC expressions.

Table 7-1   Typical LIC expressions

These expressions should be eliminated (shown by X) or written in shorter form.

Expression	Avoid	Shorten To
actually	X	
as necessary	X	
at present	X	
at this time	X	
in colour	X	
in length	X	
in number	X	
in size	X	
in fact; in point of fact	X	
in the light of; in light of	X	
is a person who	X	
on the part of	X	
a majority of		most
a number of		many; several
as a means of		for; to
as a result		so
at the rate of		at
at the same time as		while
bring to a conclusion		conclude
by means of		by
by the use of		by
communicate with		talk to; telephone; write to
connected together		connected
contact		talk to; telephone; write to
due to the fact that		because
during the course of		during

Table 7-1   Continued

Expression	Shorten To
during the time that	while
end result	result
exhibits a tendency to	tends to
for a period of	for
for the purpose of	for; to
for the reason that; for this reason	because
in all probability	probably
in an area where	where
in an effort to	to
in close proximity to	close to; near
in connection with	about
in order to	to
in such a manner as to	to
in terms of	in; for
in the course of	during
in the direction of	toward
in the event that	if
in the form of	as
in the neighbourhood of; in the vicinity of	about; near; approximately
involves the necessity of	demands; requires
is designed to be	is
it can be seen that	thus; so
it is considered desirable to	I/we want to
it will be necessary to	I/you/we must
of considerable magnitude	large
on account of	because
previous to; prior to	before
subsequent to	after
with the aid of	with
with the result that	so; therefore

Table 7-2   Typical overworked expressions

a matter of concern	in the foreseeable future
all things being equal	in the long run
and/or	in the matter of
as a last resort	it stands to reason
as a matter of fact	last but not least
as per	needless to say
at this point in time	on the right track
attached hereto	par for the course
conspicuous by its absence	please feel free to
easier said than done	regarding the matter of
enclosed herewith	the stage is set
for your information *(as opening words)*	this will acknowledge
if and when	we are pleased to advise
in reference to	we wish to state
in short supply	with reference to
	you are hereby advised

Avoid Words That Antagonize

Certain words — or combinations of words — can have an adverse effect on readers. If you use them you may never realize you have created a negative reaction. For example, if Peter writes to Chris: "I am sure you will agree that," Chris's emotional reaction probably will be *not* to agree! Consequently, you need to tread very carefully before you use any expression that may prove to be even mildly antagonistic. Such expressions fall into three groups:

1. **Words which make a reader feel guilty**

    You have overlooked section 14.

    You have neglected to sign your cheque.

    You have failed to fill in previous employment details.

    You ought to know that refund claims cannot be accepted after 30 days.

    You have not understood the specification.

Each of these expressions can make readers feel you are accusing them of being inadequate or incompetent.

Exercise 7-4

Removing low-information-content expressions

Delete or shorten the low-information-content expressions in the following sentences. In some sentences you may have to rearrange the words slightly.

1.   Should you experience further trouble in connection with your Internet account, please feel free to call me at any time.

2.   It has come to my attention that the Ardmore Account contains an error of considerable magnitude.

3.   For your information, we have transferred your account to our Regina office.

4.   This report brings the Merton project to a successful conclusion.

5.   Subsequent to a check of our records, it has been found that you have actually been billed twice.

6.   With reference to our analysis of the data printout, it can be seen that the end result was in the order of a 3.6% decrease.

7.   The employees at the Willowdale office exhibit a tendency to work more overtime than the employees who are located at the Montreal office.

8.   There is no advantage at this point in time in trying to identify who was responsible for the error.

9.   I am in the process of submitting only an approximate cost estimate due to the fact that there are too many variables to permit me to calculate an exact price.

10. In order to complete the changeover by January 31, it was considered necessary by the executive committee to employ three temporary data input operators for a period of three weeks.

Turn to page 149 for suggested answers.

2. Words that "talk down" to a reader

    You must understand our position.

    We have to assume from your letter that you will not be requesting an interview.

    I must request that you attend a meeting in room B101 on February 13.

    Undoubtedly you will be purchasing a new unit.

    We simply do not understand how you reached this decision.

3. Words which challenge or provoke a reader

    Your demand for a refund has been denied.

    You must return the form by May 28.

You have erred in completing the form.

We must insist that you comply with the requirements of paragraph 28(a).

We are sure you will agree that the return-to-work legislation is justified.

Select the Right Word — And Spell It Correctly!

Some words are so similar, it's easy to confuse them. For example,

affect and *effect*

there; their and *they're*

defective and *deficient*

auxiliary and *ancillary*

disinterested and *uninterested*

Each has a different meaning; so the correct word must be used in the proper context.

If, when you write, you are not sure whether you have chosen the right word or spelled it correctly, consult a dictionary. We suggest one of two Canadian dictionaries:

- *The Canadian Oxford Dictionary* (Oxford University Press: Toronto, Ontario, 1998).

- *Funk and Wagnalls Canadian College Dictionary* (Fitzhenry & Whiteside: Markham, Ontario, 1989).

The chief difference between these dictionaries is that the Oxford dictionary tends to favour British and French spelling (e.g. *centre; labour; manoeuvre*), while the Funk and Wagnalls dictionary tends to favor U.S. spelling (e.g. *center; labor; maneuver).* In Canada, we see both spellings daily in our newspapers, in magazines, and on television, which creates a problem: which should we use? (Many Canadians, while at school, may have experienced being taught by an English language arts teacher who contradicted the way their previous year's teacher preferred them to spell such words.) Historically, we have inherited the British way of spelling, but logistically — and by our proximity to the United States — we are exposed more often to the U.S. way of spelling.

Our advice: it really doesn't matter which you use, providing you are consistent within the same document. If you write predominantly within Canada, then the Oxford dictionary probably is for you. However, if you correspond frequently with clients or businesses in the U.S., then the Funk and Wagnalls dictionary probably is the better choice. For this book, we have chosen to use *The Canadian Oxford Dictionary* as our style guide, so you will see *theatre* and *honour* spelled with an "-re" and an "-our." We were also particularly influenced by the dictionary's genuine reflection of Canadian culture through its inclusion of numerous specifically Canadian expressions. And we liked that it's *contemporary* (it was first published in 1998).

How closely do *you* need to depend on a dictionary? If you are not sure, we suggest you test yourself by selecting the correct words in the sentences in Exercise 7–5. Then compare your choices with those listed on page 149.

Forming Abbreviations

When a long word, such as *counterclockwise,* or a multiword expression such as *document design centre,* is used repeatedly in a letter or report, it's convenient to abbreviate it to a shorter form. You can abbreviate a word or expression in any way you wish, providing

---

Exercise 7-5

Selecting the correct words

In each sentence below, identify which is the correctly spelled word or the correct word for the given circumstance. Do this without referring to a dictionary, then compare your choices with the list at the end of the chapter. If some of these (and other) words give you trouble, in future, refer to a dictionary.

1. After a (lengthy/lengthly) discussion, the committee agreed to (develope/develop) a new marketing strategy.

2. A (separate/seperate) invoice is to be prepared for each shipment to the Montreal office.

3. The (amount/number) of houses sold this year was 37 (fewer/less) than the quantity sold last year.

4. By (lightening/lightning) the workload, I hoped to achieve better employee (morale/morals).

5. (Similarly/Similarily), the storekeeper is to record (receipt/reciept) of each shipment on the blue copy of the (relevant/revelant) purchase order.

6. Although the supervisor had been (discreet/discrete), the staff (implied/inferred) from her enquiries that there still was a problem.

7. My car was (stationary/stationery) when a taxi skidded into it.

8. Although Marion was keen to hear the labour board's decision, she really was only (a disinterested/an uninterested) observer, because she would not be (affected/effected) by the result.

9. When the Manager of Human Resources tried to (council/counsel) the employees, she also asked questions designed to (elicit/illicit) information from them.

10. Canada needs a better business (enviroment/envirorment/environment/enviornment) to encourage its (entrepreneurs/ entrepeneurs/entepreneurs).

Turn to page 149 for suggested answers.

you first tell your readers what the abbreviation means. The first time you use the word, spell it out in full and then show the abbreviated form in brackets immediately after it:

The development of new worksheets and computer reports is to be monitored continually by the document design office (ddo). As each change occurs, the ddo will...

The following guidelines apply to the forming of abbreviations:

- Never form a new abbreviation for a word or expression that already has a recognized abbreviation. For example, readers probably would not recognize the abbreviation *apx,* if you were to use it instead of *approx* as the abbreviation for *approximately.*

- Use lower case letters, unless the abbreviation is formed from a recognized title such as Royal Bank (RB), or is derived from a person's or an organization's name. For example, write kilogram as **kg**, but kilohertz as **kHz** (because the first letter of Hz represents a person's name: Hertz).

- Omit internal periods from an abbreviation unless the abbreviation forms another word. For example: write **RRC** for Red River College and **CBC** for Canadian Broadcasting Corporation, but **in.** for inch and **a.m.** for morning. If the abbreviation happens to be the last word in a sentence, then the abbreviation will end with a period.

- Do not add an "s" after plural abbreviations of quantities; treat them in exactly the same way you would for a singular abbreviation, as in **34 km** and **17.4 kg**.

Inevitably, there are exceptions to these rules. Traditionally, **No.** (the abbreviation for *number*) has a capital N. Similarly, in the electronics and computer fields, VCR and RAM are always written in capital letters. Two of our other books — *Communicating at Work*[1] and *Technically-Write!*[2] — contain extensive glossaries that define how many terms should be abbreviated.

Writing Metric Symbols

The rules for writing, typing, and printing SI (metric) units are rigid but straightforward, with many of them parallelling the rules for writing non-metric expressions:

- Type all metric units in upright type, even if they are in a sentence that is set in italic type.

- Use lower case letters for all symbols, except where the letter used in a symbol is formed from a person's name: **g** for gram, but **V** for volt (derived from Alessandro Volta).

---

1   Ron Blicq, *Communicating at Work*, 2 Ed. (Scarborough, Ontario: Prentice Hall Canada), 1997.

2   Ron Blicq and Lisa Moretto, *Technically-Write!*, 5 Ed. (Scarborough, Ontario: Prentice Hall Canada), 1998.

- Always leave a space between the last numeral of a quantity and the first letter of the symbol: **20 kg, 120 V.**

- Do not add an "s" after a plural symbol: **23 kL.**

- Do not place a period after the symbol, unless it ends a sentence (see **23 kL** immediately above).

- Use an oblique stroke (/) to represent per, and a dot at midletter height (•) to denote that the symbols on either side of the dot are multiplied.

Writing Numbers Correctly

When you write numbers in a table or as part of a column, you align them at the decimal place, one above the other. When you write them individually as part of a sentence, the rules change slightly. The basic rule is straightforward:

- Spell out numbers from one to nine.

- Use numerals for 10 and above.

However, there are several exceptions you need to know:

- Always use numerals for
    - dimensions, speeds, tolerances, radio frequencies, etc.: **5 km/hr,**
    - any number that is followed by a unit of measurement: **3 mm,**
    - any number that contains a decimal or a fraction: **44.6, 2.5, 2 1/2,** and
    - percentages, sums of money, book or document chapters and page references, and peoples' ages.

- Always spell out
    - any number that starts a sentence (or, better still, restructure the sentence so the number is not at the beginning), and
    - any fraction in which the whole number is less than one: **two-thirds.**

Here are three additional guidelines:

- Always insert a zero before a decimal that is less than one: **0.67.**

- Spell out one of the numbers when two consecutive numbers are not separated by punctuation: **Thirty 80-kg** cartons.

- When a series of large and small numbers appear in a sentence or paragraph, use numerals for all of them: In room **207** there are **4** tables and **16** chairs.

Answers to Exercises

Self-Test Exercise 7-1

Changing passive voice to active voice

The following sentences are tighter and stronger than the original sentences.

1. The chairperson adjourned the meeting at 4:30 p.m.

2. At Viking Insurance, an automated answering system has replaced the manually operated telephone switching system.

3. At its October meeting, the executive of the company's social club agreed to hold the Christmas Party on December 16.

4. Mavis Barnes wrote the product analysis report, Vic Darwin edited it, and Rachel Gagné illustrated it.

5. When Revenue Canada audited Vancourt Business Systems, they found a $30 000 discrepancy between reported and actual income.

6. We recommend adopting the Westport Travel Insurance Program.

7. A 4-hour power outage caused a work stoppage at 1:55 p.m. At 2:30 p.m., the office manager decided to send all employees home for the remainder of the day.

8. The staff development committee decided to approve Terry Rozak's request to attend the April Canadian Business Society meeting.

9. Although the Steering Committee predicted a 17% loss of production for August, Production Control reported the actual loss was only 6%.

10. I am concerned that your company has faced a similar interface problem to the one our I.T. department has identified.

Exercise 7-2

Run-on sentences and sentence fragments

Punctuation problems in these sentences have been corrected. Your answers may differ slightly, depending on the approach you take with each question.

1. The red warning label on the bottle read: "Do not give to children weighing less than 30 kg." The medication was definitely not intended for 6-year-olds.

2. I have examined your Nabuchi model 400 Bubble Jet printer. Repairs will cost you $88 plus tax.

3. We installed a twelve-line telephone system, although right now we need only eight lines. Four lines are for a planned expansion next year.

4. I am requesting that you transfer my account from your branch at 1620 Portage Avenue to your new branch at 310 St. Mary's Road. This confirms my telephone instructions of May 31.

5. I have confirmed my telephone order to lease a new service van in a purchase order detailing price and delivery dates.
   Or
   With reference to our telephone call about leasing a new service van, I have originated a purchase order detailing price and delivery dates to confirm the order.

6. Please book a flight to Toronto for me on October 16, with a return flight on October 20. I prefer an aisle seat.

7. Effective June 1, Shirley Watzinger is to be transferred to Accounts Payable. This confirms my telephone instructions of yesterday afternoon. Her salary and benefits will remain the same.

8. In yesterday's email you described a problem with stationery shipped to you last week against purchase order 2720 and Invoice 1514A. The stationery was received wet and unusable. I am replacing the order and shipping it with Zipper Courier, who will pick up the original shipment.

9. We finished work on the data conversion project March 12, three days ahead of the scheduled completion date: we had a cause to celebrate!

10. The order from Nesbitt Industries came in by courier at noon on May 27. They had been trying to fax us for three days, but the fax line was not connected properly.

Exercise 7-3

Correcting faulty parallelism

The parallelism in the following sentences and short passages has been improved.

1. If we buy only three units, the cost will be $187 each, but if we buy eight or more units it will drop to $165 apiece.

2. We selected the model AS800 microprocessor because of its small size, high speed, and long battery life (4.5 hours between charges).

3. A questionnaire was distributed to customers in the Southwood Mall not only to assess the public's reaction but also to draw attention to the new product.

4. The main conclusions drawn from the company's job-sharing experiment show that job sharing

    • demands supervisors' cooperation,

    • requires compatible participants,

    • improves employee attendance, and

    • increases individual productivity.

5. When we test-ran the new series of Soapscreen 30-second television commercials before an invited audience, 64% of the general public who viewed them reacted favorably, but only 18% of the media specialists were complimentary.

6. All supervisors are to attend a ten-hour St. John Ambulance course during which they will be given training in administering first aid and recognizing and helping heart attack victims.

7. On the first day of work, each new employee is to have a medical examination in the morning and is to attend a three-hour company orientation seminar in the afternoon.

8. Jeff Freiberg is to coordinate the project, Candace Swystun is to assume administration responsibilities, and Hal Kominsky is to initiate a study of the documentation process.

9. We have purchased three dozen calculators: 25 model 70s for each assessor at $24.50, 4 model 70s to be held as spare units, and 2 model Z90s for the auditors at $38.90 each.

10. The recent downsizing has meant reducing staff by 17 employees, of whom 3 elected early retirement, 4 chose to be transferred to the Brighton office, 8 chose retraining, and 2 (Millie Yousof and Connie Doucette) selected job-sharing.

Exercise 7-4

Removing low-information-content expressions

The following examples have been edited to reduce wordiness.

1. If you experience further trouble with your Internet account, please call me.
2. I have noticed that the Ardmore Account contains a large error.
3. We have transferred your account to our Regina office.
4. This report concludes the Merton project.
5. Our records show that you have been billed twice.
6. Our analysis of the data printout demonstrates that the result was an approximate 3.6% decrease.
7. The employees at the Willowdale office tend to work more overtime than the employees at the Montreal office.
8. There is no advantage in trying to identify who was responsible for the error.
9. I am submitting only an approximate cost estimate because there are too many variables to calculate an exact price.
10. To complete the changeover by January 31, the executive committee decided to employ three temporary data input operators for three weeks.

Exercise 7-5

Selecting the correct words

The answers below will help you understand why each word is correct. If some of these words gave you trouble, in future know to refer to a dictionary any time you are not sure.

1. **lengthy, develop**

2. **separate**

3. **number, fewer**
    Use *amount* and *less* when referring to quantities you cannot count, and *number* and *fewer* for quantities you can count.

4. **lightening, morale**
    Lightening means to make lighter. *Lightning* refers to an atmospheric discharge of electricity. *Moral* refers to personal strength of character and the ability to differentiate between right and wrong. *Morale* refers to the general contentedness and state of motivation of a person or group of people.

5. **Similarly, receipt, relevant**

6. **discreet, inferred**
    Discreet means to have discretion. *Discrete* refers to two separate entities. A person who speaks or writes can *imply*; a person who listens to or reads something can *infer* from what they have heard or read.

7. **stationary**
    Stationary refers to something that is not moving. *Stationery* refers to paper products like writing paper.

8. **a disinterested, affected**
    Disinterested means to be uninvolved, unbiased, or impartial. *Uninterested* means to be not interested. *Affect* is a verb. *Effect* is a noun.

9. **counsel, elicit**
    A *council* is a body of people. To *counsel* means to give advice. *Elicit* means to find out. *Illicit* means illegal.

10. **environment, entrepreneurs**

Index